What you need to know

- Anyone can have mild to severe symptoms.
- Older adults and people who have severe underlying medical conditions like heart or lung disease or diabetes seem to be at higher risk for developing more serious complications from COVID-19 illness.

Watch for symptoms

People with COVID-19 have had a wide range of symptoms reported – ranging from mild symptoms to severe illness. Symptoms may appear 2-14 days after exposure to the virus. People with these symptoms may have COVID-19:

- Fever or chills
- Cough
- Shortness of breath or difficulty breathing
- Fatigue
- Muscle or body aches
- Headache
- New loss of taste or smell
- Sore throat
- Congestion or runny nose
- Nausea or vomiting
- Diarrhea

This list does not include all possible symptoms. You can find the most up to date list at cdc.gov

Designed and Published by Vincent Whitney.
Editors: Vincent Whitney, Shelley Malenowski

To my reader—

If you are looking for a book that will reveal to you the dark underbelly of medicine, this is not it.

If you are looking for a concise story, this is not it.

This story is told from my perspective, day to day, while I worked in the COVID-19 ICUs of New York City between April and July 2020. The names have been changed to protect the privacy of the individuals involved, but the stories are real. I have tried to simplify language and situations as much as possible to make this story more accessible, so any mistakes are my own.

You will find that characters in our story will phase in and out in the same way that they did for me while I cared for the real people they represent, so you will learn what happened to them in the same way I did.

It is the true story of a pandemic and the people that lived—and died—during it. I am just the witness.

1.

I am standing at Henry's bedside, and he is crying.

He leans into me, frog-legged, sitting up in the bed, and I can hear his sobs through his BiPAP mask. I wrap my arms around him and hold him. He clings to me as if I am a life raft. I can feel not only the hitching, hard breaths but the vibration of his fluid-filled lungs against his back.

I am crying, ugly crying, so hard I can see the fog around the edges of my goggles. I am sweating through my clothes and isolation gear, he is hot to the touch, but he leans into me, head to my belly, and I give him the only comfort I can. It's hard to imagine I have only known him a few weeks but in this moment every second is an eternity. I count his breaths, I can feel him struggling. I can't stop crying.

I know it's scary, Henry. But I promise I am going to

keep you safe. You're going to go to sleep, and it's not going to hurt.

The doctors are ready and they look to me. *Should we go get someone else?*

I think I should start from the beginning.

2.

I t is February of 2020 when I first hear about COVID-19. Some kind of virus that is spreading around China. Downplayed by major news outlets and the government, it sounds a whole lot like a cold. I am not afraid. In many ways it seems to be happening in a parallel universe from my own—sunkissed ballrooms and palm trees, I couldn't be farther from lockdowns, meat markets, and hospitals. I continue teaching at the dance studio where I work with my husband.

I have worked as a ballroom dancer for nearly 3 years—worlds away from my education and work history as a registered nurse. We joke about it. Flight prices begin to go down and my husband says, We could go to Paris! I tell him to wait.

We have vacation time, he reminds me. *We should just go.*

Earlier in the year we planned to go see a Broadway show in New York in March, on a weekend we thought we could see the cherry blossoms, but we hadn't yet booked the tickets. It is his Christmas gift to me, this romantic weekend getaway, exactly the kind of gift I would want.

In March, it seems that the virus has crossed the borders into the US and I feel the first flickers of fear. My birthday comes and our friends come over but joke about "social distancing." My husband is terrible at surprises, so he planned a surprise party and told me about it at breakfast. This is the second time in our relationship he has told me about a surprise party he has planned—pretend to be surprised! He is sheepish but elated.

It's endearing that he cannot keep a secret, especially one he thinks will make me happy. I laugh about it—he is sweet—and we gather in our kitchen with a cake brought by our friends and bump elbows instead of hug. Isn't it funny how all of your significant memories of a home will happen in the kitchen or the bedroom? Our friends bring food (It was a surprise, this was part of the plan) and in usual fashion we sit around the kitchen table for hours, talking, before we head out to the couches in the next room.

We are playing video games in our living room and laughing together, one of our friends tells us she is moving back home to Minnesota, across the country. I wonder now if I will ever see her again.

Everyone has a drink and we sit around the room with party games. There is laughter, there is joy, but there is a kind of heaviness here that we have never had before and can't quite explain. I don't have any idea now when I will see them again.

We go back to our lives at the studio for a couple of days but as the numbers begin to pour out of New York City and the reports come back, I feel a knot in my stomach: twisting and growing slowly, a live thing like a snake, it feels like it will consume me. I go to the owners and tell them we have to close the studio. We could be a vector for infection; this is not socially responsible; some of our students are elderly and could be a very high-risk population—and we do close our doors in spite of the heaviness and uncertainty we feel. When the studio closes, we discuss the strain on the business. The owners do not know how we will pay our staff with the studio dark, they do not know for how long we will be closed. we all hope against hope that it's only a couple of weeks. There is a strain on every small business during this time but I imagine that they could never have anticipated a future in which our business, teaching dance, would be unsafe to run. I certainly could not. We do not know what the right answer is but we cancel our classes and the teachers pack their things. Two of our students mention being sick this week and I wonder to myself, coldly, if it is already here.

When one of our teachers, who is an ex-pat, asks me how bad it will be, I tell her she has time to go home to her family in Bulgaria but if she is going to go, she has to go now. I don't know how I know, but I can feel the storm brewing. The studio closes only two days before the stay-at-home order is passed in our county.

I receive a call from a nurse recruiter—she has a job for me, only a couple weeks, quarantining cruise ships in California. It is the same day we close the studio and it feels like providence. It is a department of health job, No one has any symptoms yet, she describes it as *cushy*. I accept and pack my suitcase—the next day the contract is on hold as military hospital ships are going to New York and many nurses are re-routed.

It is the middle of March. We are home together for the longest time we have ever been home together with no obligations—weeks, the first time in the years we have been together. My husband and I work and live together as well as manage multiple businesses: all of which are shut down due to the pandemic. We both teach dance at a studio I manage, we run a rental property, and we are the founders of a talent scouting agency. We never could have imagined a situation in which all three of our jobs are shut down, but a global pandemic surely qualifies as the unimaginable. We are both strong personalities and while we do end up in sync it often feels more like a planetary alignment, only happening a few times a year, say, than a regular occurrence. Maybe better to think of us as two similarly-sized, similar-in-strength horses, very determined that we know the right direction and often pulling opposite in the same harness. Less pre-determined gravitational pull, more stubborn muscle.

We are both well educated but in completely opposite spheres that rarely overlap, so our common ground must come from our shared interests, passions, and work. We both know it to be the case but enjoy the challenges we bring each other, so I do not know what to expect while we are essentially unable to work and on lockdown in our home.

It is the happiest time of my marriage. My husband is more patient and understanding than I have ever seen him, there is no room for arguments or conflict in our home, and we start to talk about what comes next for our family. I am the wife I wish I had been for our entire relationship.

I think of our wedding, our first anniversary only a couple of months behind us. We are together on the beach, hand in hand, there is an altar wrapped in white linen. The beach is nearly deserted, there is no one in attendance but a justice of the peace and a photographer. There is a slight breeze, the sand is white and I can hear the waves lapping the shore.

It is perfect.

The script of our life together has been flipped and I am starting to realize this will have a much larger impact on our life than I expected.

I think of nursing school, nearly 10 years ago, my first semester when I got the first "C" of my life and was crying, thinking I would never make it and maybe I wasn't smart enough or capable enough to be a nurse. I live in a city in upstate New York that has its city streets switch parking twice a week so the snowplows can get to both sides of the street in the winter. I am crossing the street to move my car so I don't get a ticket, still feeling useless, when I see a book, a magazine, something in the street. I still don't know what possessed me to pick it up, but I did. It's a children's coloring book titled, *You can be a Nurse!*

I still have it.

I begin to remember what it was like to work short-staffed with no one to help me when I was a nurse 3 years ago. I remember begging the administration for more hands to lighten the work and how rarely, if ever, we got them. Everyone pitched in, but there was a communal sense of heaviness while we worked. We were tired. Every day we were tired, and that was just under normal, day-to-day operations. I couldn't say enough good things about my nurse managers, who would often jump in and try to help out where they could, but who were essentially powerless to provide us the additional staffing we needed. Healthcare as a business model does not often consider the needs of nurses over profits. I did the math once for an average shift on my busy cardiac floor. By my calculations, the job I was supposed to do in 12 hours should have taken me 16. On my last day, the director of nursing asked me what she could do to get me to stay. *Nothing*, I told her. *There is nothing you could do now.*

What must a pandemic feel like? Is this not what I signed on for when I took my state boards? When I quit nursing to become a dancer, I carefully folded my scrubs away into vacuum-packed bags, where they have been for 3 years. They have moved with us 3 times. For what did I keep them, if not for this?

I hear on the news that they have begun recalling nurses that have retired. Surely I, as a young professional athlete, am more fit to serve on the front lines, more likely to survive, than those who have aged out of our profession and retired. I feel a strong sense of moral obligation to take the place of someone who might not make it back.

3.

I begin applying for travel jobs every day.

I get many rejections—*They want someone with recent experience, and you haven't worked as a nurse in 3 years.*

I laugh, but it is mirthless, the sound of disbelief.

This is a pandemic! Isn't it 'all hands on deck'?

The recruiters issue various canned company responses. I am watching cases rise and the death toll on the news.

I tell my recruiters, *Submit me to the hospital anyway. Pretty soon they will take any idiot that can hold a thermometer.*

I buy a stationary bike, begin biking 20+ miles every day to build up my lungs and cardio endurance. One of my co-workers at the studio, George, my professional cabaret partner, has under-developed lungs. He has pneumonia all the time and I think of his lungs, of his heart. I call him and tell him this is important, I need him to work on his cardio endurance. He laughs at me, but I am serious. I know if he should fall ill, the strength of his lungs and heart will be the difference between life and death. He seems to be humoring me, but I cannot impress upon him how much I mean it. George is one of my best friends and I am fiercely protective of him.

The rejections continue for a week or so. I call several recruiters every day. I now am filled with a burning desire to help as I feel useless sitting at home—but also a nagging dread that this will go on much longer than we expected and I need to provide for my family in any way I can. We have savings we have worked hard for, so while we are not in the dire position that many are, I don't want to accumulate debt or tap into the money we have managed to save.

Desperate isn't the right word—but it comes close.

I get a call to go to New York City, the epicenter of the pandemic. There is no interview, only a job offer. It begins next week, Monday. This is Wednesday. I pack my bags and sit on the edge of furniture—a couch, a chair, a loveseat—for a few days and find flights and look for an Airbnb. I cannot believe how inexpensive the flights are, and my husband strongly encourages me to fly first class for the first time in my life. I submit my flights for reimbursement, I message a dozen Airbnbs within a mile radius of the hospital. I settle on one, only two blocks away, and book. In order to ward off the inevitable panic, I meticulously GPS my Airbnb location to the hospital, to the nearest grocery store, to the subway station. I study my old nursing textbooks, taking obsessive notes. I repack my bags for the third time. We go to the grocery store and I buy toiletries for the next three months, as if they will not exist in New York City.

The fear tiptoes delicately in, as if on pointe, lightly creeping, a mist, almost as if I could miss it. If I am not paying attention it will be close enough to smother me. With the death toll seeming so massive, Medscape has dedicated a page just to medical staff that has contracted the virus and died. I scroll through the list of names in disbelief. There are so many, people with families and dreams and ideas and futures, reduced to names on a list. It seems obscene.

I buy life insurance. Funeral costs can be expensive and the last thing I want is to burden my husband with burying me with a portion of our savings. I think how cruel it would be, to leave this for him to worry about.

At least, I think, this is happening now, instead of July. July is when all the new medical school students graduate into their residency as new doctors and are allowed to practice medicine. I often spent the first years with an intern or first-year resident teaching them skills such as how to work IV pumps or inject medications; while they were often brilliant minds they lacked real-world medicine. That's what residency is for. One of my dearest friends began as an intern at the hospital I worked at and spent a great deal of time on my floor for 2 years. She was a bright, idealistic young resident who graduated to attending and became a brilliant doctor. She jokes still that I taught her everything she knows.

At least it's not July.

I miss dancing—it feels like an ache, but our studio owners tell us the studio is not to be used for any reason, so we cannot go there, lock the doors, and dance as we might have before.

George and I practice normally 4 or 5 times a week and we have not danced in at least 3 weeks. We were invited to perform at a show in a few months, but I wonder listlessly if the show will even happen.

I begin to pace. I buy masks, not exactly the med-ical-grade ones but something close. I buy goggles. A student asks me to meet her at the studio. She is a physician here at a local hospital. She has packed a care package with medical-grade masks (a couple of them, all she could spare), a box of gloves, lotion, fuzzy socks. Comfort in as much as she can think to provide.

I am genuinely flooded with gratitude for her compassion, for her thought. I thank her but it feels inadequate. We don't know what to say.

Saturday my husband makes my favorite breakfast. Crepes, with caramelized apples and cheese. It's supposed to be brie, that's how the restaurant I liked used to make them while we still lived in New York, but we can't find any on short notice so we settle for cream cheese. He far exceeds my expectations for homemade crepes, serving perfectly caramelized apples and toasted crepes with melty cheese.

I drink my latte and I think back to our breakfast dates at that restaurant years ago while I worked the night shift—both of us bleary-eyed but together, the mahogany tables and benches, the chalkboard menu. Holding hands over the table and drinking our coffee, he is not yet awake and I am exhausted from a long shift. He is telling me about his night, jovial, it is show and tell. He is never short on enthusiasm and he can't wait to share the new thing he was reading about that he thought was so interesting. Crepes, caramelized apples. Extra brie, salad greens. Scrambled eggs. I wonder what kind of person eats salad for breakfast and prefer to think of it as garnish.

It still feels surreal that I am leaving home tomorrow and I do not know if I will ever see my husband again.

We wander around as if we are in a dream, my dogs faithfully following me as I circle the tile floors. My husband, normally loquacious, he always has something to tell me, is quiet.

It seems as though there should be channels in which I have worn the ceramic away, as if I was a body of water through rock, so fierce do I feel. There are no channels of ceramic missing, no holes or divots in the tile from a multitude of footsteps, but the dogs are content to be included in my exercise in futility. They will stay home with my husband, although I desperately wish I could bring them with me. I know I will probably be working long hours and it would be unfair to bring them. I repack. We re-record our dance routines from the driveway because I don't know when we will dance again.

How strange it is to me that the professional routines we have danced for years, polished and worked through and sharpened and softened, will only exist in binary code, as a series of zeroes and ones, a series of movements, of expression. Instead of on my body, in the music, they will exist in a file somewhere, compressed and flattened to make space in my mind for whatever comes next.

I, a professional dancer, do not know when I will dance again.

I cry in bed, in the dark. He reaches for my hand and I hungrily try to memorize the way his fingers curl around mine, the skin of his fingertips, his callouses. Ridges in his palm, folding over my fingers, he squeezes. I remember the day feels as though it is just about to rain—darker, gray, with the air hanging heavy around us in some just imperceptible way. The photo I have from that day, inexplicably, is sunny.

4.

Sunday morning I am sitting at the kitchen table and I can't help but cry again while I drink my coffee. My flight is in three hours. My husband takes my hands and begins to tear up as well. I am afraid and I can see that he is, too. He brushes the tears from my eyes, his voice thick, and he tells me he will book me the longest massage I can stand as soon as I get home, a pedicure, a whole spa day and he will make sure there is nothing possibly I could have to do. He says we can buy the house I want to buy and he promises we will go to Paris, just next year. He begs me to come home and I hold his hands to my face, hot and wet with tears and the stink of fear. The clocks have sped up.

Empty isn't the right word, but it comes close.

He takes me to the airport and it is all I can do to hold the tears back as I deliver my bags to the drop-off and get through TSA. My voice breaks when the gate agent asks where I am going, and the agent does not charge me for the additional baggage, even though they are overweight. I wonder idly if this is because I have a first-class ticket, because I am going to New York City, or because I am crying.

In some ways, I feel like a soldier going off to war, leaving my family at home with the fear I will not make it back—I wonder at the airport if soldiers cry.

I have never seen the airport so empty. Vaulted ceilings and gold outlined fish and sea animals in the tiles, they are normally packed with people. I feel alone and the echoes of thousands of travelers from the time before are not enough to comfort me.

My husband insisted I buy a first-class ticket—it was cheap, but all food and beverage services are discontinued so essentially all of the perks of going "first-class," aside from the chair I sit in, are suspended. Are airlines' classes of service suspended? Are social classes suspended? It seems like illness and death are unimpressed by your station.

In this moment, flying into what seems like certain doom, I wish I could have a drink. I don't normally drink but it seems like the thing to do when you suspect a possible outcome of an event is your death. It doesn't matter. I can't even get a mimosa.

I have a book, but I can't read. I can't focus.

It seems like a metaphor in some way for what is about to happen, but I feel thick and dull with stress and I can't quite grasp it.

I decide to take an Uber to the apartment. Although I could try to navigate the subway, I have two suitcases, huge, they are nearly two-thirds of my body weight, and the idea of carrying them up or down stairs, of wrestling them onto a train, is daunting. The Uber driver wears a mask. There is a plastic shower curtain duct-taped between the front seats and behind them. He does not speak.

It is a different city at this point in the pandemic. The streets are cleaner than I have ever seen them, almost deserted, with every solitary passerby crossing the street to avoid coming too close; they all wear masks. Nearly all the businesses are shuttered and closed, regardless of their function. Steel grates pulled down to the ground, padlocked, it looks like the Great Depression. Restaurants. Nail salons. Retail stores. There are signs, too many to count—*No shirt, no mask, no service,* and *Closed due to COVID-19 pandemic. Hope to open when it is safe.*

I think of all of the small businesses with their lights off, like my own, and I wonder when it will be *safe,* how many of them will be lost to the pandemic and never turn the lights on again.

I make it to my Airbnb, the place I am supposed to call home for the next three months. There are three doors between me and the street—an iron gated door that locks when it is closed, a door into the anteroom, and a door into the living room.

The anteroom is small, barely more than a hall-way, with hooks on the wall for coats and a thin shelf to the left, directly opposite the door into the apartment.

There are canvas bags on the hooks in the hallway and wicker baskets on the shelf.

I unlock the door to the living room and bring my luggage inside.

There are photos on the wall I did not put there, the same artist, cities in the shape of fish, there is a rug on the floor in front of the couch, faded but clean. The couch is hard and dark blue, the same color as my couch at home. There are red pillows, a green blanket, everywhere there is color that seems foreign to me as it is so different from my own taste. There is a mantel in the living room, plastered over where once there must have been fire. On the mantel, there are small stones, stacked on top of each other. I wonder if they are glued together but in three months I never check. There are windows at the end of the living room to my right that face the street, shuttered and closed. The floor is pine, maybe, full of knots that are sanded down and very real in its imperfections. The kitchen is just a small area at the end of the living room, neat and compact, orderly with a cart against the wall with the silverware and pans. The knives hang above the stove, what you might call an apartment-sized oven, it is in miniature. The plates are in a cupboard above the stove, there is a microwave on top of the mini-fridge, and the bedroom and bathroom are through the doorway into the kitchen. It is clean.

The bedroom is bright and the sun shines through the shades and lands in pools on the blankets in the lazy way that early afternoon sun will. There is a wrought iron headboard and mounds of fluffy white linen. More decor on the walls I did not put here. I feel oddly like an imposter, a stranger in someone else's home.

The bathroom is full of tiny bottles of travel toiletries, stocked, there is nothing I could want. They are the perfect size for a weekend stay, but I am still glad I brought my own.

My landlords are a family—husband, wife, small son. They tell me that the wife and son are out of the city for now, but he is an essential worker so he will be home.

Hilariously, although the walk to the grocery store is only a leisurely couple blocks, it turns out it is uphill I have to carry my grocery bags back home. It seems I should have thought about it on the way there; I should have noticed the slight downhill slope, maybe made two trips, but I am too distracted by the suddenness of it all. I woke up 1300 miles away in Miami, and now I am grocery shopping in Brooklyn. It strikes me as hysterical in an ironic sort of way. I found reusable canvas bags in the mudroom, and am glad I brought them with me because there are no plastic bags in New York City. The bags are heavy—I have tried to pick up enough groceries to last me a few weeks so that I do not have to go out and potentially be exposed to any more virus than I will already be at work—let alone expose a stranger to it.

Is this another metaphor for the situation? I still feel too slow and clumsy to articulate it as I climb the hill, slightly out of breath. Some professional athlete. I have never lived alone in my life. I have always had roommates. I am nervous. Excited? Sad. Afraid. It is a bitter-tasting, jittery feeling.

The mask on my face feels foreign, but comforting —I take a small amount of peace feeling my own warmth in the mask and knowing it is sealed and I am not breathing unfiltered air.

I get an email Sunday night that says that the hospital uniform is navy pants and a white top or white all over and I snort-laugh to myself. No nurse I know has owned white scrubs since nursing school, and there are no scrub stores that are open right now. Nothing is open, it's a pandemic!

It feels surreal because it is such a bizarre imposition during this time.

5.

Monday, we have orientation virtually because it is too big of a risk to bring us all together and into the hospital. I learn there are a hundred and fifty travel nurses beginning this week, spread throughout five hospitals in the hospital system. There will be another hundred the next week, I will learn later, and another hundred the week after that. Notably, our uniform requirement is waived. I am glad I did not buy them, as some nurses tell me they did. They wonder aloud if they can be returned. We have to go to Manhattan for the occupational health clinic, which they spring on us in the second half of orientation. We have to go today, before 4 PM, to get fit-tested to make sure we are wearing the right size masks. I am in Brooklyn but I successfully navigate the subway alone for the first time in my life. I have been here before, but always with a companion more familiar with New York City. I feel a vague sense of accomplishment although the stations and trains are nearly empty and there is no one to share it with so it feels hollow.

There are no appointments, although I wish there were—doesn't it seem like we should have appointments for this kind of thing?

I arrive at the address they gave us in orientation; it is a skyscraper and I must take the elevator to the floor number that I can't remember. There are fewer people than I expect, maybe only 20 waiting already outside the elevators, and they take us inside the testing room in groups of 4.

Stand on your x, six feet apart. Put on the mask, the hood.

I'm going to spray this bitter-tasting chemical into the hood. Read this paragraph aloud. Do you taste it? Smell it?

No? You may keep your mask. Sign here. Have a nice day.

My next scheduled workday is Thursday, and today is Monday. I think irritably that I could have done a fit-testing for a mask at home, flown in Tuesday or Wednesday, had more time with my family.

It's funny—we have days, years of our lives with our families, so many we take them for granted. Never before have I so bitterly resented the loss of a few days. I am a skin-flint, cheap, wishing desperately to hoard more of these empty days for my family. Miserly isn't the right word, not exactly, but it's the closest one I have.

All of New York City is shut down. Time Square is empty, and the ads playing on billboards to no one are surely a statement of the times we live in. There must be some intelligent metaphor here, something about capitalism soldiering on although the world around it has collapsed, but I cannot put the words to it now.

I have two days off, but for what? I pace. The pine is not any more susceptible to being worn away by my bare feet than the tile was 1300 miles away at home. I watch reruns of The Office, without knowing why. Maybe there is some sort of comfort in watching a story I am already familiar with —a story in which I already know all the characters and how it will end when there is so much uncertainty in my real life. It is mundane and lighthearted, like potato chips for my brain. It asks for nothing, demands nothing, at any point if my mind wanders it is safe, I will miss nothing. I know how the story goes. I stretch. I go to the park, only two blocks away. I didn't think parks this big existed in New York City—the walking path might be a four-mile loop. I notice, vaguely, ironically, that there are cherry blossoms now in the beginning of April and I send a photo to my husband.

It looks like I made it for the cherry blossoms after all.

I see a couple walking their dog in the park from afar—it is a lovely, bright spring day, the flowers are in bloom and they are holding hands. They are older, silver-haired, but standing tall, backs straight. Their dog trots near their feet, impeccably heeled, he is also gray in the muzzle and the sunlight emphasizes it. They are so casual that their masks don't even seem out of place. I wish I didn't feel so alone, and I wonder if I will see my husband age like this—if I will see him again. In the movie version of this story, I would be brave, a heroine, I would stride into the great unknown. In real life, I am blown glass, so fragile I could shatter.

I meet my landlord, climbing the stairs one day as I am heading out to the park. He introduces himself and inquires about the hospital. Specifically, he wants to know if there is enough protective equipment for us. He gets a small supply of N-95 masks, not many, but some, and if I need any....

He is tentative. He knows he may not be able to give much, but he wants to offer what he has. He trails off.

I thank him and tell him I have not been inside the hospital yet but I did bring some of my own, just in case. Keep them for himself. Thank you so much for thinking of me.

I go for a run. I read more about the numbers coming out of New York City—10,000, 11,000, 12,000 cases a day when I turn the news on. Deaths are climbing, 700, 800, 900 or more in a single day. Refrigerated trucks for bodies outside hospitals because the morgues are full and completely over-run. I watch more reruns of The Office until it's finally time for bed.

6.

My neighborhood is only blocks from the hospital, historic brownstone buildings like townhouses with painted iron fences and tiny gardens that are just starting to put up green shoots into the sunlight. It might be lovely, under other circumstances, but now it looks almost abandoned.

I will later learn that it is considered very exclusive—historic brownstone!

I wish, instead, for fenced-in yards for my dogs to play in. For sprinklers, garden beds, for my gazebo at home. I wish for space.

I walk to the hospital. The air is crisp and slightly cool, the sidewalk wide but uneven in places—enough to trip on if you aren't paying attention. I notice, and approve, of the bike lane off of the sidewalk, separated from oncoming traffic by parked cars. It is painted green, with the white outline of a person on a bike.

I walk to the end of my street opposite the park, where there is a subway station, and up two blocks, past a small convenience store and many shuttered businesses. The side of the hospital I approach from passes the refrigerated trucks. There are two, sometimes three. I remember idly a superstition from my childhood about how you're supposed to hold your breath as you pass a graveyard. I remember holding my breath for what felt like forever, while my parent's car drove past lush, green cemeteries that seemed a mile long. I can't remember what the bad thing was that would happen if you were unable to hold your breath. It feels kind of like an itch in my brain I can't quite scratch, trying to remember. What was the thing that was supposed to happen? At first, I feel a vague unease as I pass by but by the second or third week I don't even glance up. It's funny what you can get used to when you don't have a choice.

Thursday I have half a day of classroom orientation in a building across the street from the hospital. I think of Miami, where all the buildings are beautiful—brightly painted, they have fountains, mosaic tile, and Spanish moss. Comparatively, this building is industrial, gray. I take the elevator upstairs to the classroom where I am shown how to work the hospital's brand of IV pumps, feeding pumps, and glucometers to test blood sugar. We break up into groups and it feels oddly comforting, like a rerun of nursing school clinicals my first semester, but compressed into a two-hour period. This is a controlled environment, there are no real patients here, nothing can go wrong. It feels safe— I feel safe.

I ask the nursing educator. *I'm a step-down nurse. Are we going to be working in the ICUs?*

I have a bad feeling that this is going to be so far over my head I might drown. (A step-down nurse might work on a "step-down" unit, a higher acuity of illness than a regular medical-surgical floor, but below the level of an ICU)

She hesitates, but meets my eyes and shrugs.

It's okay, I tell her. *I just want to be prepared.*

There is a pause, the whole room is waiting to hear her answer.

Yes, she admits. *Probably*.

I begin to understand most of the hospital has been repurposed for ICU beds due to the acuity (severity of illness) of our patients. I am in some ways relieved she has been honest with me. I am not prepared, but at least I know I have never been an ICU nurse before. There is no possible way I could be prepared for this.

Next, we have two hours of charting, which I

am anxious about as I don't recognize the brand name of the computer program. As we open it, I breathe a silent sigh of relief because it's the same charting program I used in my last hospital job. It comes in handy because we spend most of the two hours getting everyone logged in. It feels like such a mundane joke about an orientation—that we spend hours on the technology, while accomplishing almost nothing except getting everyone logged in. It feels surreal in how ordinary and predictable it is. It would feel like a waste except for the anxiety in the room, in all of us, but above us, like electricity hums in a circuit.

I go to a half-day orientation on a step-down unit. The nurse we are supposed to be shadowing, Sveta, is pleasant, but preoccupied with her four patients. We try to help her as best we can for a couple of hours, although since we don't know where anything is we are probably more of a hindrance to her. She will never say so. There are 8 beds in the step-down bay, 4 on each side in a very large room split down the middle. One side is empty at the moment, so she is the only nurse here. The step-down units are slightly higher acuity than the regular medical floors, but lesser acuity than the ICUs. Literally a "Step-Down" from Intensive Care before discharge or being downgraded again to a medical-surgical floor.

There is one patient here I cannot forget, a Russian grandmother, who, although she speaks no

English, is remarkably friendly and expressive. I squeeze her hands, helpless to do much else, while Sveta talks to her in Russian to find out what it is she needs. Her daughters work in the hospital, so although we do not allow visitors her daughters come up on their lunch breaks to sit with her. The patient was one of the few at the time that did not have COVID-19—in fact, to be allowed into the step-down unit each patient required a negative test to prove that they were safe to be in an open-air bay with the other patients. As I would later discover, nearly every hospital unit has a family member of staff, or a staff member between their pressed white sheets. She is a lucky one—most our patients, at this point, are infected with COVID-19. This one step-down unit is the last so-called "clean," unit for patients to go.

Sveta is sweet and gives us each a button that says some version of *Great Job!* or *Good Work!* at the end of our shift. She says she is passing them out to everyone as a morale booster. I wish I could in some way humanize Sveta more here but every interaction I had with her in my three-month contract was the same. She is exceedingly pleasant and unfailingly sweet—not cloying, like syrup, she is sweet like chilled fruit on a summer day, refreshing—every time I see her. This was one of my last days in the step-down for the duration of my contract.

I breathe a sigh because at least I have another full

day of orientation tomorrow, where it won't be so busy. There will be one more day I can observe the workflow of the unit, the documentation, and day-to-day before I am on my own for the first time in three years.

I come home, strip at the door and get in the shower, as hot as I can stand. I scrub my skin and climb into bed. I talk to my husband briefly—I am so emotionally exhausted I do not have much to say. It is the only time I really get to talk to him and I will come to cherish our nightly calls over the coming months. I lie in the bed, which I have to admit in spite of myself is extremely comfortable, and feel, rather than hear, the subway under the street beneath me. There is a heavy vibration, the rattle of the train tracks. It will pass by every 30 minutes for the next three months.

I don't sleep much. I can feel in my bones that I am in the eye of the storm.

7.

The next day I am with my new manager while she is finding a unit to orient me. We stop first at a step-down unit, where I see Sveta, and she waves at me, but another nurse is crying and Sveta is comforting her, rubbing her back and talking softly.

My new manager, Lisa, is a no-nonsense, motherly kind of person, and she asks why the nurse is crying.

The nurse is blonde and pony-tailed, eyes red, and she says, *It's just...I have a cough and a sore throat. I have a fever. I think I caught it. And I have asthma.* She keeps lowering her mask because her breaths hitch in her throat, she has been crying so hard.

Lisa tells her firmly. *First of all, put your mask back on.* There is a sprinkling of laughter in the nurses gathered at the desk. *Second of all, go home. Get tested.* She pats the nurse's back and gives her a one-armed hug.

But I don't want to leave them short-staffed.

Lisa shakes her head. *We will shift some staffing around. Go home.*

I think how funny it is that nurses will never change—there is a global pandemic, she may have caught the virus like so many of her co-workers and patients, and she does not want to leave her colleagues short staffed this shift.

Lisa continues her rounds and one of the ICUs is short-staffed. The nurses should have 1-2 patients each based on acuity and they will have 3 or 4. There is a pause while the manager tries to calculate who she can shift around to help. I came here to help, right? I volunteer.

Can you take a team? They ask.

Of ICU patients, they mean.

I take a deep breath. I say *Yes, as long as someone can help if I have questions.*

There is a visible relaxing of the ICU nurses gathered around us. Someone says, *Of course we will help you, we don't let anyone drown.*

I wish I remember who it was, but this day is a blur. I feel like I am an imposter but they absorb me. I am one of them.

They give me the two most stable patients. I am wildly underqualified, but this is a trial by fire and the only way out is through.

We are supposed to spend as little time in the rooms with the patients as possible in order to decrease our exposure to the virus because we think viral load, or the amount of the virus you are exposed to, might have something to do with how sick you get. We expect it will be elderly people that suffer the most but to my surprise we have many people of all ages intubated in the ICU—30s, 40s, 50s, 60s. All visitation has been cut off to the public due to the risk of spreading coronavirus in the community—we are a designated COVID-19 hospital in the area, I find out. Sometimes hospital staff may stop by on their breaks to see their loved ones—it is hard not to look the other way.

They already have to be here. Already exposed, they lie awake with the idea that they are the one that has carried the virus home with them. That a loved one may have picked up their scrubs, their shoes, carried them to the laundry. Rubbed their eyes. They have sneezed in the kitchen, quickly, unable to cover their nose, their spouse has walked by, hours later, poured a glass of water, sighed.

That they have laughed, long and loud, with a beloved spouse or parent, an asymptomatic carrier, and their loved one has breathed in the droplets containing the virus for which we have no cure.

I am given one N-95 mask, the gold standard for respiratory protection, and told that I should wear it until it doesn't work anymore because there is a shortage—if it is broken I may turn it in for a new one. I have a paper bag to store it in. I have researched the manufacturer recommendations for re-use and I know there are very few ways to sterilize them without degrading the filter. In normal times, these would be single-use—we would don them to go into a patient's room, perform our tasks, and then throw them out when we left the patient's room.

They seal around our face, with a thin aluminum strip at the top and two elastic straps. We form the aluminum to our noses and cheeks, it is held in place by too-tight straps behind our heads, there are indents in our cheeks from the sides of the mask, from the elastic.

We should not get any fresh air through the sides or bottom, no smells, nothing—they should form a seal. We should feel our own breath, warm, against our faces.

I make a mental note to bring mints.

My first day, one of my patients is on his deathbed. His family is on Facetime on an iPad, on a stand in the room. We know it is imminent and they have invoked a *Do not Resuscitate* (DNR) order because there is little hope of his recovery, especially since he has already suffered cardiac arrest once in the night prior. He is in his 60s and very gravely ill. I take a deep breath—I know I'm not supposed to expose myself unnecessarily, but no one should die alone; it feels wrong, barbaric to me somehow. Surely we must be better than this.

I stand in front of his door, don an isolation gown and one pair of gloves. I tie the gown behind my back and I don a second pair of gloves. I adjust my goggles, make sure the seal on my mask is good. I wear the booties over my shoes from room to room, and I have a surgical cap over my hair I wear all day.

I am opening the door when the resident in charge of his care walks up to me and asks what I am doing.

I'll do it, she says. *You don't have to expose yourself. I have to be there anyway to pronounce his time of death.*

I understand she knows it is my first day and she is trying to spare me the worst of it in the only way she can.

She is with him for two hours, standing at his bed-side. I am standing vigil outside through the cold glass, making sure the resident doesn't need any-thing, in between checking on my other patient. The rooms dampen sound, but are not soundproof. I hear the wail of despair from his wife when he dies—like a wounded animal, through the glass. It is a good death, insofar as one could be good in this situation—he passes quietly and gently, with his family looking on and someone holding his hand. I do not think he suffered in this moment but the noise his wife of 40 years made while she watched him die over a video call is a sound I couldn't soon forget.

This story is overlaid with codes and intubations being called approximately every 30 minutes. A code is called to activate critical care physicians and nurses because a patient's heart has stopped and they are suffering a cardiac arrest. We must intervene or they will die. In this context, *Code* is synonymous with cardiac arrest, with a heart that has given up and must desperately be coaxed back to life. There are lesser critical responses, so-called *Rapid Response Teams*, commonly named an RRT. An RRT might be called for a patient that is suddenly confused, for example, a sudden deterioration for a patient on a medical-surgical floor that requires more intensive care.

It doesn't matter—there are no more ICU beds to be had. At this point, there are no more of the standard RRT that I hear about. Every patient is critical, there are only resources for Codes—there are so many.

Chest compressions. Epinephrine. Bicarbonate?

Pulse Check. Get the backboard. Does anyone have the labs pulled up? Chest Compressions. Epinephrine. Pulse Check—Rhythm Check. Is it shockable? Clear!

An intubation will be called if a patient is experiencing respiratory failure and needs the support of artificial ventilation, temporarily, while we hopefully treat their illness and their lungs recover. Very commonly, the cardiac arrest and the intubation will go hand-in-hand. If someone requires full cardiac support to save their life we will almost always have to provide respiratory support with an intubation. However, a patient's care may also require intubation due to respiratory arrest or respiratory failure even if their heart has not stopped. If their lungs are not adequately exchanging gases, they may require respiratory support in order to save their life.

Every 30 minutes, more or less at this time in the pandemic and in my hospital, someone loses a pulse or needs a ventilator. A critical care team might vary, depending on the hospital, but will usually include a physician or multiple physicians, a critical care nurse to assist who is specially trained in this situation, an anesthesiologist who will help intubate the patient, a respiratory therapist who can assist and manage the mechanical ventilator, a pharmacist, a nursing supervisor, etc.

They stop calling the codes and intubations overhead because it is too depressing for the staff and begin to page the providers instead. We know if they are too close together, there may not be enough physicians and respiratory therapists and anesthesiologists to respond to the new patient while they are still trying to save the last one. We are working on a skeleton crew. We may get an anesthesiologist, a respiratory therapist, and a physician, but there are no critical care nurses to spare for the code team, let alone pharmacists. There are not enough warm bodies to help. There are two ventilators left in the hospital and we have an algorithm for the Emergency Room for whether or not we can use them on a patient who comes in. This is what disaster triage looks like.

It feels surreal. I am working, but as if in a dream; I see my hands performing tasks, but they do not feel attached to me. It doesn't feel like this is really happening—like must be a dream from which I will wake up. Out-of-body isn't the right idea, but it's close.

It takes me 3 or 4 days before I feel confident I can keep an ICU patient alive by myself. I have never taken care of ventilators or titrated medications like this before. I feel wildly underqualified still but experience my first sense of accomplishment when a patient is critically ill and I am able to stabilize him myself by adjusting his IV medications including sedation, blood pressure medications, and pain control, which we commonly call "drips." This is in my scope of practice as an ICU nurse, and although in normal circumstances I would have an orientation months-long to teach me this, it is a crash course.

During normal times, we have IV pumps for every patient, every medication, in order to appropriately control medications and fluids and be sure patients are getting the correct amounts of each. The pumps are programmed with our drug library so there can be little mistake—the pumps usually even know the correct rate for the medication. There is little room for error.

Now there are not enough IV pumps for all of our patients, so they are relegated to the ICUs. The pumps are to be used only for "high alert" drugs, which is almost everything we give in the ICU, requiring precise dosages and calculations we cannot trust to drip-rates. Controlling blood pressure, controlling heart rate, and rhythm. Sedation. Pain killers. Anticoagulants. Electrolytes that can cause cardiac arrhythmias if they are given too fast, but must be replaced or the heart will surely fail. Bicarbonate to control the pH of the blood. Some of these ICU patients will require as many as 10 IV pumps each. We have nothing to cure them—only to prolong this fugue state, to support their bodies in the hopes that there will be a miracle. One day at a time.

Nurses on regular medical floors are using drip-rate calculations and counting drops from the IV tubing chamber, controlling the amount of drug with roller clamps on the IV lines. There are no pumps for them. This is the end of the world, I think. It feels like war-time—none of us have done that kind of thing since nursing school. This is a first-world country. How can this happen?

8.

I sign up for as much overtime as I can, my second week, working 6 and 7 days a week. When I am working I don't have the time to be afraid—and they desperately need the help, so they take me. I sit home on my days off and wonder if I am going to get sick—if there will be an anesthesiologist or a code team to intubate me if I need it. I miss my husband so much. I can only imagine the things I haven't done with him yet, and I cry. We haven't gone on a real vacation in years because I didn't want to take the time off of work, my fault, he begged me to go.

I wake up in the morning. There is no coffee pot in the kitchen, only a French press. I have been told it is supposed to be better but at 5 am it's not a thing I care much about. I open the coffee, stick my nose in the bag—I can still smell it. I breathe a sigh of relief.

I lie in bed, by far the most comfortable place in

my rental apartment, with white linens and down comforters. I feel the fluffy texture of the duvet, the cotton under my fingers, the softness, and I marvel at the threads that hold this together. It's funny, when I was at home I never felt like I had enough time—I managed 3 companies, interviewing people in the morning before practice and scheduling a cleaner for our rental property in between teaching and practice and travel. I worked 70-80 hour weeks and while I loved what I was doing, I never did feel like I had enough time—time was a luxury.

Time is all I have now, while I am alone here in the New York City apartment, burdened with what was once a commodity. Unless...I don't have time. It feels like the calendar has been compressed somehow to a desk calendar, a single day per page you'd tear off, but I cannot see the stack of days underneath. I do not know how many days are left in the year. In my year.

I haven't met our children.

I am not done dancing.

I cry.

I go back to work.

9.

My second week I overhear the residents discussing patients in their daily rounds. They have three patients that need dialysis urgently on their list, but only one dialysis machine to spare—there are only 10 for the whole hospital. The fellow, or the resident in charge, is a kind, patient man who I respect immensely in my brief dealings with him so far. Grimly, he says they have to dialyze this patient first because they are the most likely to survive. The residents square their shoulders and nod, and they remind me in this moment of children at a funeral.

Dressed up in their white coats they become children carrying a weight far too heavy for them, a burden they should not have to bear, but impossible to be helped. They are all adults, but none of them feel ready for this. None of us are.

The hospital begins to provide meals to the staff,

3 meals a day, and I give up trying to prepare meals or worry about my macros: something I paid close attention to back when my body was my job, as a dancer. Grams of protein, grams of carbohydrates, calories mean nothing to me. I eat whatever they bring. It's one less chore I have to worry about. I am unsure if the hospital is paying for them or if they are donated. I know there have been a great deal of donations. I decide I am grateful, but too tired to care to whom.

I arrive home one day, taking my shoes off in the anteroom, to find a plastic bag on the shelf outside my door. There are N-95s, three of them, clean and unused. I am so touched by my landlord's kindness, knowing he only gets a couple of them for himself and he has left some for me.

My heart feels raw at the kind of selflessness he has demonstrated, while I know he is an essential worker and he is also at risk.

I get up in the morning and fill the French press. I pause to stick my nose into the bag of coffee.

I can still smell it.

I go back to work.

10.

We extubate a patient, only the 6th one since the beginning of the pandemic and the first one I have witnessed. The attending physician in charge of the residents looks at them, says he knows it is risky, but he can't stand it. If we don't extubate anyone he's going to go home and shoot himself. There's a spattering of laughter, uncertain, he tells it like a joke, but I wonder sluggishly if he is a little bit serious.

The residents gather outside the room and watch through the glass and we all clap when the patient coughs and sputters and breathes on his own. Extubation is a high risk for aerosolizing virus particles, particularly dangerous for spreading infection, so the only people present in the room are the attending physician and the fellow. The rest of us huddle around the window together, like a sports team of some kind waiting for the coach to call the game-saving play. It feels like a miracle and for this one moment, we breathe a collective sigh of relief. His wife watches on a video call, and I hope she can hear us cheering for him through the door. When he becomes well enough, we downgrade him to a medical floor. As far as I know, he made it out.

My father is hospitalized for chest pain days later and, although we have not been close in years, when he texts me I am at work and I cannot stop the panic rising like floodwater under my skin. If he is hospitalized there is no chance he will not be exposed to this virus—by patients, by well-intentioned healthcare staff who do not yet know they are sick.

He and his wife are in a high-risk group, and I am terrified they would not survive should they contract COVID-19. My eyes are burning while I text him that if his EKG comes back normal he needs to go home—he can follow up outpatient. I tell him to wear his mask the whole time, no matter what.

He is discharged, safe, and a voice in the back of my mind begins, quietly, to say something I haven't yet fully let myself consider.

What if there is not a dialysis machine, a ventilator, an anesthesiologist left for me?

While I am in this unit I care for a patient, a woman in her 50s who has Down's Syndrome.

Madelyn was COVID-19 positive, survived her extubation, and is breathing with minimal support on a nasal cannula. Her hair is gingery, thin, and she wears wire-rimmed glasses. She is a miracle. I feel grateful to be caring for a patient that has survived the worst of it. Her sister is a pediatrician who has video calls with us and her. She tells us that Madelyn is the reason she went to medical school and obviously loves her dearly. I leave them to visit with the iPad and when I come back in to check on Madelyn her sister is playing piano for her and singing. Her piano playing is simple and her voice is only on key, but in the moment it is beautiful to me. While I am leaving, Madelyn says to her sister, *I love you.*

I feel a headache coming on. I go home and in spite of the Tylenol I take I can't shake it. I sleep. Sleep always helps.

My head still hurts. I fill the French press. I stick my nose in the coffee. Is the scent fainter, or is it me?

11.

One day I am working in the same ICU and am off the next day. The next shift is short and I offer to stay an extra 4 hours, until midnight, to help. The nurse I am supposed to be giving report to on my patients is late. She is from Endoscopy, used to doing procedures on stable patients. It's a funny phrase, "Give report," but that's how we say it. I have never thought about the origins of the phrase, but that's how it has been taught to me.

I am still waiting to give her report on the patients, to hand off responsibility, when I see her talking to the nursing supervisor just off the unit. She is crying, her face red. She comes to get her assignment from me, dejected, it is clear to me that she is telling them she cannot do this, she is not qualified, she does not feel comfortable or safe. It is my turn to help.

I'm not an ICU nurse, she tells me. *I'm an Endoscopy*

Nurse. I have never worked in the ICU.

It's my turn to mentor someone, which seems ridiculous, I have been an ICU nurse for a couple of weeks, but I try to be comforting.

I won't let you drown, I tell her. *I'm here until midnight.*

We have a patient I have dared not move all day, he is so hemodynamically unstable—his blood pressure is so labile I am afraid I will cause him to code simply by changing his position and turning him on his side. She wants to give him a bath, a real bath. She wants to do things right, and I appreciate her for it. He was stable today, I think, without being repositioned, maybe we can if we are careful. We wash the front half of his body, whatever we can reach, and change his gown. We lower the head of the bed, cautious, so we can turn him on his side and wash his back, but his blood pressure plummets and he looks gray.

She looks horrified, sheet white, and I spend the next 30 minutes stabilizing him. We are a team. I don't leave until 12:30 am.

After a few weeks in a real ICU, I am deployed as a float nurse throughout the hospital to many of the "field ICUs" that exist. We did not have enough ICU beds—so we made more.

There is a painting outside the unit where I spent most of my time in the hospital, six feet wide and in watercolor. It features a nurse, standing tall with a stethoscope and a cape.

We will find a way, or we will make one, it says.

I know it has probably been there for years, but it seems like a sign of what is to come.

Every operating room (OR), every recovery room (PACU), every room we are not using has been converted to a mobile ICU unit, staffed with critical care nurses, and with stacks of supplies on the walls. We don't have another choice. The emergency room cannot handle the influx—we have patients on gurneys in the hallway because there is nowhere else to put them. We have stopped all elective and non-emergent surgical procedures so we can repurpose these rooms.

Gone are the days that we were *not supposed to expose ourselves.* I sit in the OR bay with COVID-19 positive patients for nearly 12 hours. There is no other place I can see their makeshift monitor setup. They have set up "Negative Pressure" in the rooms, with HEPA filters, which are supposed to constantly be filtering the air in the room and sucking particulates out, but we are suspicious about their effectiveness and are reluctant to trust their makeshift solution. It's not that I blame the administration—it is an impossible situation requiring ingenuity—but I don't necessarily feel safe. Does anyone? I think of the Broadway musical *Hamilton*, of the phrase *Rise up.* It takes me a few weeks before I feel comfortable saying that I did rise to the occasion, but I aspire to. I know if I do not, people will die.

I walk into the nurses' lounge to get a bottle of water where another nurse is eating an orange. I think how much I love the smell of citrus, tangy and sweet—oranges smell like summer, to me, like sunshine.

I haven't taken my mask off.

I panic internally—I can smell the orange. I have been in the PACU bay all day with COVID-19 patients and my mask does not work. Well, what's done is done, I tell myself. I have been in there, six hours exposed and I didn't know it. Nothing I can do now will change it. I find the nurse manager and ask for a new mask.

She seems suspicious. *Yours looks like it's in working condition.*

I tell her about the orange.

Her eyes widen and she takes my arm. She brings me out of the PACU, almost dragging, she tells me if it happens again I should stop what I am doing and get a new mask immediately. She gives me one extra mask in my size and I store it greedily in my paper bag like a child hoarding candy.

12.

My first day off in nine days, I plan to drop off my laundry at the dry cleaner and make breakfast. There is no laundry in my apartment and I only have one day off before I go back to work for another 9 days in a row. I signed up for the overtime voluntarily, and I do not complain—but I know it is an inhuman number of hours to work and I am exhausted.

When did it become *my* apartment? I can't remember.

It is only 8 AM and I walk to the nearest dry cleaner that is open, nearly half a mile, and drop off my laundry. My landlord recommended a dry cleaner just down the street, but when I arrive there is a sign, *Closed due to COVID-19*, and the nearest one I can find is the one I walk to.

Once I am back, I turn on the gas stove and begin to warm up some frozen spinach. I realize the trash needs to go out and without thinking, I take it outside. The outermost door swings closed and I realize my keys and phone are inside. I am locked out.

I knock on the door to my landlord's apartment, which is up the stairs above me. He does not answer. I have hardly slept in over a week and I cannot process what is happening. My brain feels jumbled with abstract art, as if the pieces do not quite fit and I cannot assemble the thoughts to see what they are trying to say.

I see a woman on the street walking her dog, a stranger, and I tell her what happened. I do not know what to do. I cannot get in any other way. I have lived here for less than two weeks. Is it the third week? Maybe this is the third week. I don't even know what day it is. I am locked out in a foreign city. Logic would dictate that I should call a locksmith but I have no way of calling anyone or contacting anyone including my landlord. The stove is on. I am panicking. She suggests I go to the coffee shop at the end of the street, ask to use their phone and call the fire department. I do, she walks with me, and they give me the phone. I call the fire department and they arrive within minutes. I am mortified, in tears, apologizing, panicking, helpless, exhausted. I tell them there is no fire, (yet) while they open the fire hydrant nearest to my house. Water is gushing into the street and they look annoyed. The firemen are able to use an axe to pry open my outer door without breaking it (although it didn't latch quite as well after that) and laugh their whole way in, boots traipsing through my clean apartment. They turn off my stove.

You didn't even burn the spinach.

So much for independence.

The hospital begins to provide scrubs to all of the ICU units to wear so that they are not bringing Coronavirus back home to their loved ones. Initially, I try to pick out scrubs that look nice or might be well-fitting. Maybe a color I think will be flattering. After a few days, if they are even close to staying on my body without falling down or splitting, those are the ones. Anything more than that is useless energy I am expending. It takes me a few weeks to get into a rhythm, but eventually I begin to take a clean pair of scrubs home with me. I wear a pair of leggings and a shirt under the scrubs I bring home because I find out the hard way I am allergic to the industrial detergent they use. At the end of my shift, I walk out in my leggings with new scrubs in my bag and the dirty ones left in a hamper to be washed by the hospital. I wipe my pens and scissors down with a disinfectant. I wipe my phone down, my scissors, my ID badge.

When I arrive home, my shoes and bag stay outside my apartment in the anteroom.

I get up in the morning, fill the French press. I can

still smell the coffee.

13.

It is maybe 3 weeks into my 13-week contract and I am sitting in another OR bay with COVID-19 positive patients. They are all ventilated and sedated, like almost all of my patients are these days. One's heart stopped at 7:30 AM on the dot, during a shift change. A shift change is a terrible time for something to go wrong. There is no one available to help necessarily, as people are coming, going, reporting off to the next shift. The night nurse is exhausted. The day nurse knows nothing about this patient except that they are currently, clinically, dead.

The patients, in my experience, rarely consider the shift change.

He was coded—we tried to save him, but were unable to get his tired heart to beat again. The clock has stopped. We call the morgue to pick up the body, clean him, and cover him with a sheet. We sit in the OR bay with two sedated patients and a dead body for 6 hours while we wait for the morgue. I remark on it at the time—that it's strange what you can get used to when it feels like the world is on fire. God, my back hurts. Come to think of it, my legs are sore—kind of a general ache.

It's hard to be so afraid when you are sweating through 3 layers of clothing and PPE and 2 layers of gloves. My protective gear—isolation gowns, scrub caps, N-95, surgical mask, goggles, and gloves over my clothes seem woefully inadequate next to the hazmat suits I have seen from other countries—but we don't have anything else, and there is nothing to be done.

We are out of booties and disposable surgical bonnets, or at least they are not widely available, so I do not have them.

I wonder, vaguely, if the lack of appropriate PPE here means we are considered less valuable here than nurses are in other countries.

The morgue comes and we get a call that we must get an admission who requires an emergent intubation. The bed is still wet with bleach. Javier arrives, in his 60s, white-haired and pale under his tan. I ask him what his name is, what his birthday is, he is able to tell me while he struggles to breathe. When we get him on the monitor I can see that although we are giving him as much supplemental oxygen as we can, his blood oxygen saturation is only 70%, while it should be above 90%. I am amazed he is still conscious, let alone alert and oriented.

The anesthesiologist is able to get his consent for the intubation, since he is still able to make the decision for himself. Javier signs.

Do I have a choice? He wheezes, shrugs.

I hold his hand and he squeezes. We push the sedation and paralytic through his IV so we can intubate him, and his hand goes limp in mine. They intubate him, he is hooked up to mechanical ventilation, and we set up his IV medications.

Realistically, almost all patients on mechanical ventilation, especially when they are unstable, require sedation. It must be a terrifying experience, to have breaths drawn for you forced down your throat through a straw. Often, they will breathe on their own, out of sync with the ventilator, and in doing so will actually fare much worse, decrease their oxygenation, and exhaust themselves. They will only be awake while intubated if their medical team thinks they can handle a breathing trial or extubation. I am grateful that they sleep. I think that being awake and on a ventilator sounds like a special kind of hell.

Today, I meet Jake, a spectacular critical care nurse who works as a part of the float team for the hospital. He tells me about his boyfriend, about his family, his mother, his condo. His mother wants him to have babies with a nice girl. He thinks that maybe his relationship with his boyfriend will "go the distance." His boyfriend works in marketing and design—no, *it's really supply chain*, he corrects himself. It is the first human interaction I have that is not about fear in a month. He becomes a pillar of stability for me throughout the months I work there—while he generally has a dark, dry sense of humor, he is very peaceful, zen. Jake does not feel stress, he channels it, and he is an incredible asset to the team but he will never admit it. He will often busy himself running and fetching and helping the other nurses if he is not active—there is never a time someone else is busy that Jake is not. When he is sincere, he is remarkably kind, but he cannot take a compliment in return. Every day I work alongside Jake I feel less anxiety because I know if something goes terribly wrong he will be there to help, because that's the kind of nurse and person he is. He will go on to work in the unit I worked in most frequently for the majority of the time I was there, it seemed, and we were better for it.

When he asks me how much money they are paying the travel nurses, I hesitate, but I tell him—I know it's much more than he is paid. I feel vaguely guilty, but having left my husband, my home, to do the hardest job I have ever done in my life—I feel like I am earning every red cent; simultaneously, I am certain that Jake and the other staff nurses deserve it just as much, if not more, than I do.

He tells me that their contract as staff nurses does not include hazard pay, although some hospitals are paying it, and he is trying to work with union reps to get hazard pay approved at our hospital. The conditions under which they worked at the peak of the pandemic were unthinkable and it leaves me with more respect for the nurses still standing after the initial onslaught before the travel nurses arrived. They do eventually get a small bonus—twice—but I will later hear that approximately 30 staff members have died of COVID-19 since the beginning of the pandemic. A security guard. A painter. Nurses.

I hear staff members talk about how the information they had changed so much—in the beginning, they were told not to wear masks around the hospital. The virus is spread by contact, not by droplets. It's not aerosolized. You don't need a mask. It's not a good look for the hospital. Inciting panic. That's the official statement from the hospital administration.

Written up for it, they resorted to peeling their flu stickers off their badges. That was their excuse. They didn't get a flu shot so they were required to wear a mask, that's the hospital policy.

People began to get sick.

Masks were okay, Hospital administration announces, but they did not have enough N-95 masks and the ones they had should be conserved. A surgical mask was sufficient unless it was a procedure like an intubation that could generate a lot of aerosolizing particles.

People continued to get sick. The policies changed every day.

One night I am leaving I hear the nursing supervisor say that 60 critical care nurses have called out sick tonight.

I understand that the money they are paying us, to travel here to help, is blood money.

The fear comes in waves now—predictable, like the tide—but it is not a constant, nagging thing like pain. I am too busy, too tired for fear, and every day I do not lose a patient is a victory in this war we are fighting.

14.

I see my reflection in the mirror at some point, time is irrelevant, there is only work and not work, and realize I have bruises on my face from where my goggles hit under my eyes: little half-moon wedges of darkness. We know that many procedures will aerosolize virus particulates, so even my eyes must be protected. The goggles are so tight that they cut into my cheeks and forehead but I don't care because it is safer that way.

I try to wear a silicone strip on my nose to protect the skin on my nose from the pressure of the mask, but sometimes having the silicone prevents a good seal on my mask. It's not worth it. My nose is reddened with broken skin and sore. I wear the mask for my entire shift, 12 hours, because I do not dare take it off.

I realize my head hurts again.

I look so much older.

George calls me and I ask him if he is safe, staying home, being careful.

I am. Not as careful as you'd be though. I'll never be as careful as you'd be. He laughs, a little guilty.

I remember my job before, as a dancer. It seems laughable—like another world. I miss feeling beautiful. I think of rhinestones and self-tanner and contouring powder and eyeshadow palettes, all staples of my competition routine, and they seem like artifacts of a different era. As if one day, archeologists will find eyeshadow palettes and excitedly share them in museums like shards of pottery, so many colors. They seem so ancient and past.

15.

It may be that a month has passed since I have arrived in New York. I'm so exhausted that time seems irrelevant—I don't even know what day of the week it is. We run out of a medication we are using to sedate the ventilated patients, hospital-wide—so everyone has to be changed over to a new one. Now. I wonder how it can be possible that a hospital has run out of a medication. We call the physicians, ask them to reorder the new medication, wait for the pharmacy to approve the order. Get the medication, prime the IV tubing, program the pumps.

I begin to see acquaintances and colleagues and family and friends post things on social media about "what's really happening" with the pandemic, conspiracy theories accusing healthcare workers of being crisis actors, etc. I begin to argue with them, to tell them what is actually happening in my ICUs, but eventually give up.

I am tired. I feel betrayed that they would watch conspiracy videos from strangers instead of listening to me, someone they know and trust, who is living this. I wonder how they could say these things about healthcare workers—nurses, doctors, therapists. I wonder if they remember me when they say them, think to themselves that I am the exception, or if they write me off with the rest of the faceless, nameless humans they do not know break their backs to be called *Monster. Actor. Liar.*

I have a telehealth visit with my therapist. I strongly suspect every healthcare worker coming out of the pandemic will be diagnosed with PTSD. There is so much death around us and we are helpless.

My therapist agrees—she seems overwhelmed. Normally, she is a talkative person. She brims with suggestions, challenges your perspective.

Today, she is mostly silent. These are the sickest patients any of us have ever seen and there is no solace she can offer me. We do not know what the future holds. Appointments with a therapist these days are hard to come by—two weeks booking out, at least, she tells me. She has a waitlist.

Around this time the hospital has completed renovations on their former psychiatric wards so that we have additional ICU capacity, but in one place. It allows us to pool resources like respiratory therapists and physicians so they can all be available for critically crashing patients.

They hope to begin surgeries again as soon as the wave has subsided and will need the PACU and OR bays again. We think it is too soon.

I become one of the regular staff on this unit, working here nearly the rest of my contract. It's makeshift at best—there are exposed pipes in every room to retrofit the medical air, medical suction, etc that each patient needs. The nurse managers are the former nurse managers of psychiatric care, so far out of their element they must also be tired and overwhelmed but they give us a pep talk every morning at the staff huddle. There are only a handful of facility staff that are available on the unit at any given time—mostly it is staffed by travelers, like me. There is camaraderie, we are in this together. We recognize each other and we form our own team. It is makeshift, in some ways, like me. *Rise up.*

There are monitors for the patients in the rooms that sync up to a monitor at the front nurses' station. The station also has cameras with live feeds into all the patient rooms so we can see them when we are not physically with them, as there are no windows or glass in the remodeled psychiatric unit doors.

You can tell a lot about a nurse, about a person,

by the way they treat powerless people when they think no one is around. I make my best friends here by watching the monitor while I am waiting for the monitor nurse to eat her lunch. As I cover her post, I watch the heart rhythms of our patients and the nurses in their interactions with them. I see a nurse gently washing a patient, carefully she arranges his limbs to reposition him. She places a pillow under his head and arms, and she strokes the hair back from his forehead. There is a pause, she considers, and she puts a pillow between his knees. I know her outwardly to be tough, abrasive —but here, alone with her patient, she is soft.

I don't know what I expected.

I make more friends than I can explain this way, watching them with their patients and knowing we are cut from the same cloth. They are people I can trust. We are one.

The rooms are nearly soundproof so often we depend on the monitor nurse to radio us and tell us there is a problem. We carry walkie-talkies with us and often the monitor tech will re-direct us if there is a pressing issue in another room. *Ellie, your blood pressure in 79 is a little soft, it keeps dropping. It looks like your pump is not running.*

Roger. I'll head in there now.

The walkies make me feel like a child at first, playing at a war game, but they quickly become just another tool and the awkwardness dissipates. This is how we communicate in a nearly sound-proofed ward. How we get the help we need to our bedsides, how we save lives.

We have some nurses who were pregnant working with us. We don't know how the virus can affect them but we do have a couple pregnant women in medically induced comas with the Coronavirus.

I hear stories of a woman that had to be intubated, pregnant, she is maybe 6 months along. When her intubation was called the OB/GYN team came, afraid they would need to do an emergency c-section because she would not survive. They did not have to this time, but it feels almost parasitic; they use the word *harvest,* I know they mean to save but I cannot shake the images that it conjures. *Harvest.*

I am glad the C-section does not happen.

My husband mentions to me that maybe we could have a baby sometime soon. He sounds wistful at the idea of being a father. We both want children, someday. I do not tell him about the emergency c-section that almost happened. *Not yet,* I tell him. I think of maternity wards, pastel and bright, of nurseries, of N-95s and isolation gowns, hospital-acquired infections. My skin crawls like so many fleas, lice, some kind of microscopic insect I cannot name. *Not yet,* I tell him.

We keep our expectant nurses at the monitor to limit their exposure to the virus. It feels like we are protecting them. From what? We don't know exactly, but we all feel it. We keep them there, safe, in their glass nurses' station bubble, as if we can will them to be healthy by keeping them behind us; we use our bodies as shields from the unknown.

Anne is a critical care nurse who used to work on the code team. She is a strong nurse and incredible resource and I imagine how terrifying it must be to be pregnant during a pandemic. She never cracks. She sits at the monitor like our guardian angel with a white, flowered headband, wide, that has big pastel buttons for her mask ear loops. She is radiant somehow, in spite of the pandemic, her belly so big in front of her, it is the only part of her that shows. Juxtaposed next to this scene, so full of life, she is beautiful.

I am sitting with her one day, watching my patients' vital signs and cardiac rhythm, and we are talking about the situation. She sounds sad for the first time. She says, *You know, in the ICU, we are used to death. Maybe we lose a third of our patients. But... not death like this....*

I can only listen. I haven't been an ICU nurse during normal times. I don't know another way. I think of life growing in the midst of all of this death. It feels wrong, but somehow hopeful.

I go home. I fill the French press and stick my face in the coffee—I can still smell it—right? It's the way it's always smelled. It's still coffee, just farther away. That's why it doesn't smell so strong.

16.

We get the preferable medication we like to use for sedation back and we switch the patients all back again. Find the residents. Ask them to reorder it. Wait for the pharmacy to approve it. I get it from the pharmacy, I prime the IV tubing, label it, reprogram the IV pump. I hope I can get it dosed appropriately before the patient begins to wake up.

My studio calls me and explains that although they told me initially they would continue to cover my health insurance while I was gone, that they will instead be laying me off and no longer covering it. I don't blame them, although I feel hurt—it felt as though they were trying to support me and now that support has been revoked. Unreasonable, but I can't help it. I could ask them to put me on my husband's insurance and change our policy to a family plan, as he is still an employee but my boss mentions it is more expensive than individual coverage. I sign up for coverage through my travel company, which I am thankfully still eligible for on my only day off in two weeks. I understand that this is an enormous financial burden, the insurance, as their dance studio cannot operate. I am still sad, as if the last vestiges of belonging to this family have for some reason been stripped away. What is a dancer who does not dance?

I am resentful that I am dealing with this my only day off in two weeks.

I can no longer see my regular therapist with my new insurance, and the idea of meeting a new one is overwhelming so I don't. Avoidance isn't the right word—but maybe it is.

At this point, each ICU nurse (including, laughably it feels, me) is assigned a "helper" nurse most days who can fetch and run, pass medication, help with patient care, etc. That is how sick these patients are, that in some cases there must be two of us simply to survive another day. Some of them are wonderful, brilliant nurses who are a pleasure to work with. Some of them are psychiatric nurses, formerly of the very same unit we work on, repurposed from one thankless job to another.

I have given up on limiting my exposure to the virus. I have seen plenty of patients with pressure ulcers, giant, necrotic wounds sometimes in patients that have been bed-bound and ventilated for long periods of time, caused by the pressure and weight against the skin for long periods of time without rest. The skin is starved of oxygen, blood, nutrients, compressed between a bed surface and bony prominences, and will begin to break down to open wounds, pressure ulcers. I try hard not to pass judgment, as I know in this time many nurses have been working with patient ratios that did not allow them to provide the basic care they needed—only to keep them alive.

At some points, at the height of the pandemic, ICU nurses who should have 1-2 patients reported having as many as 6 or 8. Running from bed to bed to make sure each patient's blood pressure and oxygenation and sedation were adequate, refilling IV bags, drawing blood, suctioning the mucous plugs out of breathing tubes. Running. Chest compressions, begging the heart to beat. There is no one to help. Your patient's sedation drips have run dry. They are waking up. Trying to pull out their breathing tube. They are afraid. Clocks tick by the second hand instead of the minute, there must be so much noise. I am surprised none of the nurses went insane. There is no way they could do what needed to be done, no way they could do anything but the bare minimum to keep them alive.

There is more time now, more staff. I turn the patients, rotating them every two hours to prevent ulcers. I wash them and brush their teeth.

I get into a rhythm.

At 7:30 AM, we have our staff huddle, conducted by the nurse managers.

Thank you for being here, for leaving your families and your homes to come work with us. If you need anything let us know. Let's have a great day.

During one of our morning huddles, they announce we are allowed a new N-95 every day. I cannot believe it. Clean masks. Greedily, every day, I arrive on the unit and take a new mask. It seems bizarre that in the time before I might have used twelve in a single shift on a single patient. Wasteful. I have to remind myself that this is the way it is supposed to be, the cleanest, safest way, that this is only temporary, a crisis. It seems like it has always been like this, safety is an afterthought for us now, our goal is survival.

We get our assignments, patients divided out like tangible weight we will all carry, the responsibility we share. I get report from the night nurse. I see my patients, assess them, and document their assessment in the 8 o'clock hour.

I turn them my first time seeing them, listen to their heart, their lungs, their bellies. Check the level their endotracheal tube is at to make sure they are appropriately ventilated. Check the medications that are hanging and that they are appropriate based on the orders, IV medications expire every 72 hours, check their IV sites, feeding tubes, their skin. I chart all of this.

Do we have an order for a urinary catheter today?

It's almost 9 o'clock. I pull the medications I need to give them, any extra drips they might need on standby. I label their IV lines. Chart their vitals and their input/output so we can keep track of their fluid balance.

I crush their medications and put them down their feeding tube. Check the feeding solution and make sure they do not need more, that it is labeled and dated and timed. Brush their teeth.

10 o'clock vitals.

Input/output. Plan for the day. I ask the physicians for any orders I might need for patient care, ask them what they need for the day. Blood sugars.

Turn.

11 o'clock maybe I can give them a bath and brush their teeth. Vitals. Intake and output.

Wound dressings?

12 o'clock vitals. Intake and output. Medications if they have any. Adjust their drips if I need to.

Now is a good time to start dialysis if we have to. Call consults we might need to follow up on, read through old orders, and clarify. Turn.

1 o'clock I might get to read their histories. Vitals. Intake and output. I will need to do care plans, document education: deferred, my patient is unresponsive and I cannot teach them about health promotion—not today. Organize.

2 o'clock is time for the next turn. Vitals. Medication. Blood sugars. Intake and output.

You get the idea. It goes on until 8pm.

I go home, strip everything off, shower. I wake up. I fill the French press. I can still smell the coffee. I go back to work.

17.

Almost all of our patients in the units I work in at this time are COVID-19 positive, intubated, and sedated. We try every possible solution to avoid intubating our patients including high-flow oxygen and BiPAP in the hopes we can preserve their lung function with some positive pressure—intubating them is our last resort to prevent brain injury, cardiac arrest related to blood gases, to prevent certain death, and every single intubation feels like a failure. It feels like we fail a lot.

I meet Laura, intubated and sedated, she has a history of MS and a few other pre-existing conditions. Her husband works here and he calls every day. Laura is pale, dark-haired, and tangled. She has a scab on her face from the adhesive from her breathing tube holder breaking her skin down. We call the breathing tube holder an AnchorFast. I notice her hair against the white sheets—so stark it looks like someone has turned up the contrast on our lives.

She is not doing well but my other patients are sicker at the time so I don't see much of her today.

Our patients will never ask us for breakfast or tell us it hurts. I feel like a sentinel, a guardian of the gate and beyond. They are my charges to protect. I memorize their histories, their prior illnesses, their current labs. I commit their "normals" to memory so I know when something seems off. I wash their hands and shave the men's faces when I can, which is not often. I know where they are bruised and I anticipate their needs. I have new IV drips at the ready for when this one runs out. I meticulously sign, date, initial each wound dressing—I label the IV tubing with dates and times. I set up stopcocks to bridge medications that are compatible together and I label the tubing again with the drug nearest to the patient so if there is an emergency I can easily identify what I need. I give them extra blood pressure medications when I know I am changing positions and adjust their oxygen levels to anticipate an increased need while I am turning and positioning them. I prepare tube feeds and spare everything. I advocate strongly for treatments I think would be beneficial and I feel some days that I have kept them alive with sheer force of will and Norepinephrine. My "helper" nurse some days ends up caring for our more stable patient while I frantically try to pull the other back from the abyss, re-wind the clock just a little, just enough. These are the sickest people any of us have ever seen.

I know our mortality rate for intubated COVID-19 patients at this point is 90%. I understand that my care is therapeutic for me, not for the patient in many cases. I do it anyway.

There is a gentleman on our unit we are caring for who is not doing well—Sergio. Redundant isn't the right word, but he isn't doing well—and just like the rest of our patients—there is nothing we can do for him.

Sergio's family has shown up here once already, snuck up onto the unit, one of them had a knife. *How did they get here?* He says if Sergio dies he will come back and shoot us all. We call security. The security officer shrugs. No one seems to know how they got here, or to be very worried about it.

I have heard the other staff say they are a part of the mafia. I might have laughed but I could see from their faces they were serious.

The physicians explain to the family that Sergio is not doing well. I can hear the clock tick, and we have to call a code.

It is nearly 5 PM in the evening when the family shows up downstairs. They have already threatened us once; our nurse manager says they cannot be allowed upstairs for everyone's' safety. I feel sorrow for them, for how this must feel—to lose a loved one behind closed doors—but I am also frightened.

We code Sergio three times before the end of our shift. We get a pulse back. He will go into cardiac arrest again overnight, but they get a pulse back, too. His grasp on life is tenuous, his fingers slip as he dangles over the abyss and try as we might, he cannot hold on. He will never make it.

The residents explain to them that he will not recover. They make the decision the next day, abruptly, it feels, to make him a DNR and withdraw care.

They are on Facetime, taking notes and photos. We remember their threats and we are afraid. There is nothing we can do. We call security to post an officer outside the unit door.

At 3 PM I notice the security officers are gone. I call security and demand they send someone—at shift change, no one came back. The family is most likely to act out after Sergio's death, I tell them, now is the highest risk for staff. They have already been here, threatened us. The officer comes back, standing guard outside the doors, and the clock stops. We call the morgue.

For some reason, we have an in-service on a new kind of cooling blanket instead of active shooter drills.

The stress is palpable, the entire shift we wait for things that could go wrong. Codes, active shooters, what else? We make it to the end of our shift unscathed; no one comes.

18.

I am reading medical journals about promising treatments, frustrated by the futility I feel around me. Why aren't we trying those? In my irritation, I ask an attending physician as she passes by a barrage of questions about treatments we aren't trying. My hands are on my hips, I am accusatory, I demand answers. She has dozens and dozens of patients to see.

She stops, she turns to me, and she leans back against the wall in the hallway. She is long and lanky, her curls are wild, and she doesn't seem at all frustrated, instead she is kind. She owes me nothing, this strange nurse that has accosted her, but she gives this gift to me of time.

She systematically explains—*We tried this medication. This didn't work. We tried this but there was another study that suggested it would increase mortality. We tried this ....*

She goes on to answer my questions in the time she doesn't have to spare.

It just seems like nothing tips the scales one way or the other. The people we thought would live, live. The people we thought would die, die. She has been doing critical care for 20 years, she has never seen anything like this.

Doctor. What are we doing? What's the plan?

She smiles at me, the kind of tired, sad smile that you know has seen a great deal of suffering recently.

Well, my dear, she tells me, *The best and the brightest minds we could find all sit in a boardroom every morning while we try to figure that out.*

Everything we do thus far is supportive therapy while their bodies fight. We will breathe for them. We will filter their blood. We will regulate their body temperatures and blood pressures and oxygen levels and electrolytes while we hope they can hang on long enough to fight it off.

Overwhelmed isn't the word, but it comes close.

This is the first time in my medical career or education that we didn't *HAVE* a plan. A treatment. A course of action. That there was not an answer. It must be May.

19.

I am at the monitor when I see they are performing a bedside procedure, sterile, the patient is covered in a blue drape and they are at his head. He is intubated and sedated in a medically induced coma, our patient, he does not mind the surgical drape. Anne tells me they are performing a tracheostomy, a surgical breathing tube, bedside.

It is taking a long time.

Something is wrong.

The patient's heart rate is dropping, dropping, it is 30 right now and we surely will have to code him, it seems like there is a lot of blood, I open the door.

How can I help?

I catch sight of the same attending physician with the wild curls. Immediately I am calm. She has it under control.

We are able to stabilize the patient, of course we are, the nurse in the room is pushing drugs into his IV under the sterile field, how could we not with this doctor?

Later, I ask the physician what happened. She clasps her hands. *When we began the surgery and we opened his throat, his breathing tube and trachea were both so encrusted with mucus and secretions, we couldn't tell where one ended and the other began. We had to re-intubate him.* She seems frustrated, helpless. She did her best. She has performed this surgery a thousand times before.

His clock ticks on.

I go home. I smell the coffee. I wonder if everything tastes bland normally. I go back to work.

When did it become *home*, I wonder?

20.

I am sent to step-down for a single shift and I realize the Russian grandmother from my orientation is gone. I ask where, and a nurse tells me she was diagnosed with COVID-19 and she has been sent to one of the regular ICUs.

At the end of my shift, I go to see her. Her daughter is outside the glass doors, eyes wet. *What happened?* I ask her.

She was diagnosed with COVID. Her daughter tells me, her voice breaking. *I just signed the DNR. It does not make sense. She would not survive.*

Tick, Tock.

I hug her. I cannot imagine the burden she, or any other essential worker feels at this moment, feeling as though they may have been unwitting carriers of this virus to someone they love.

None of the other patients in the step-down unit, I

would come to find out, nor any of the staff, tested positive. I am grateful, selfishly, that at least that my family is at home, in Florida, far away from this.

I go home. I watch reruns of The Office from the faded, clean carpet in the living room. I can feel the rug, fibrous, rough under my feet, I am sitting with my knees draw up, back against the couch. I revel in textures now. They are the only kinds of things I can feel with my skin.

21.

I am assigned to Laura again, the patient I cared for only a few days (weeks?) ago. Her husband works here—I thought surely she would die, another tragedy, with her hair against the pillow so dark it seems like someone must have upped the contrast on the photo.

Today she is awake, with a surgically inserted breathing tube in her throat called a tracheostomy. She almost weaned off of the oxygen support completely, but she cannot yet speak. It is less traumatic, long term, and safer to have a tracheostomy, than being intubated. She works with physical therapy and they get her up to the chair, first thing in the morning—it can't yet be 9 AM. She is crying sitting here, and immediately I am on high alert. I ask why and she mouths to me, *It feels so good.*

I think it's funny the kinds of things we take for granted and I get better at reading lips as the day goes on. We have dozens of funny, frivolous conversations while I try to understand what she says, voiceless. She laughs at me, joyous that someone has the time to try.

I smile and try to comb the tangles out of her hair, weeks old, they are matted to her head in places. I dote on her—this day, she is alive. She is awake. She is a symbol to me of hope in this moment, that for all of the death I have seen there is life.

The sand in her hourglass is endless. She has a fifteen-year-old daughter whose birthday is next week. Laura tells me she has never missed her daughter's birthday before.

She begs me to cut her hair.

I will butcher it, I tell her. *I do not know how to cut hair.*

Please, she mouths. *It hurts. It's matted. It's tangled. It gets caught. Please. Cut my hair. It will grow back.*

I wrap her in a towel to catch the hairs.

I do cut it off with my bandage scissors, cautious at first, but eventually giving in as she directs me, *Shorter.* She is relieved when I comply, face relaxing, although in some places the hair she has left is only two inches long.

I tell her I want to shave her face. She has grown some chin hairs and she is only 40.

She tells me, *No, I get them waxed. Can you pull them out?*

My other patients are stable. I begin to pluck some of them out with the tweezers I got from a suture kit. They are awful. I get a couple of hairs out in one good pull and she blinks hard.

Ouch! She mouths. I am getting much better at reading lips, today.

Sorry, I say, *I just am having a hard time grasping the hairs with these tweezers. I figured while I had them...*I am still focused on her face, but she reaches up and touches my hand, pauses.

She looks at me out of the sides of her eyes. *It's not like they are going to run away.*

We laugh, the windows on one wall face out into the city and there is sunlight pouring through them. For this moment, there is a sense of normalcy.

Another nurse comes into the room, brings Laura something. She turns to leave and Laura looks at me.

She mouths to me—*If I close my eyes, will she go away?*

Laura! I am shocked but can't help but laugh and she knows it, mischievous, she grins. I am in love in this moment with her spunk, her attitude. She is so *alive*.

The speech therapist comes and is able to fit a speaking valve onto her tracheostomy.

Say your name, she tells Laura.

Laura cries when she hears her own voice again, a hard break from her mischief earlier.

I thought I would never talk again.

Can we call my family? I want to tell them I love them.

Hope isn't the right word, but it comes close.

22.

I am home on my day off one morning and all I want is a latte. I go to the corner coffee shop, where I have ordered one ahead for my walk in the park. The barista sets it on the table in the doorway, eyes fixated on my face, he steps backward quickly as if I am a leper. He smiles at me nervously under his mask but says nothing. I think it's strange, but I turn to go. As I take a sip of my latte I realize I forgot my mask. Embarrassed, I hurry home. I keep extras in my anteroom and I have to get one before I can go back out.

One of the nurses I work with worked as a nurse during the AIDS pandemic. *Does it feel like deja vu?* I ask her one shift while we both have a moment to catch our breath.

No, she tells me. *This is worse. At least during the AIDS pandemic, we knew fairly early on how to avoid it—we didn't feel like we were at risk. Now...every time I walk into a room I am afraid.*

I learn how to do a specific kind of dialysis we use in the ICU called CVVHD. We use the dialysis to take the place of failing kidneys, to filter the blood for our patients that cannot filter their own. I have never done this before. I learn how to use cooling blankets. (These are much less complicated). I learn to manipulate arterial (A) lines, set up for bedside medical procedures, to replace electrolytes according to protocol. To manage diabetic Keto-acidosis with hourly blood sugar checks, insulin drips, and anion gaps. To run blood gases on an i-stat machine and interpret them. Things I haven't done ever in my nursing career and haven't studied since nursing school 10 years ago. In order to cope I become compulsive about learning everything I possibly could to make me a better nurse.

Nothing seems to taste like anything.

My walkie crackles.

Ellie, you have a phone call, line one.

It is my 90-year-old patient Betty's grandson on the phone. His mother has decided to withdraw care for Betty, knowing she will not recover when we remove her breathing tube (extubate). Betty is 90, and she has lived a good life, her daughter says, she understands the ramifications of her decision. Her grandson is my age, an adult, and he has called me to ask for an update on her condition.

Did you talk to your mother? I ask, gently. I don't want to tell him anything he isn't prepared for.

She told me to call you, he says, gruff. *Have you seen people in her condition get better? People her age get better?*

It's not impossible, but I would say very highly unlikely. The doctors have to give an official prognosis, would you like me to go get one for you?

He sighs. *I don't want the doctors. What's going to happen when they remove her breathing tube?*

I pause. I know what he is asking.

Sir, to be honest with you, I expect she will die. But... this kind of life, kept alive by machines, is this the kind of life she would want to live? Is this enough life for her? I understand it seems hard, but we are not here to judge.... Think about whether or not this is the kind of life you would want for her. She is in the ICU. If she can hear us, she can't respond. We poke her, we prod her, we move her at all hours of day and night. Constant tests. She has a feeding tube. This is not a life, She is only being prolonged here.

He is quiet, the gruffness gone. His voice is soft. *I understand ma'am. Thank you for being honest with me.*

I replace the phone, softly in the cradle, Jake is at the desk.

That was nice, Ellie, he says. *Gentle.*

I think instead, I wish Betty's grandson was rude, I wish he was angry. I wish he did not thank me when I told him that his grandmother would die.

I think of my own grandmother, of how I might feel if I was told she would die tomorrow, as if we could set an expiration date like old milk from the grocery store. I am hollow.

The days pass. I go home. I smell the coffee. I go back to work. Occasionally I get packages from home and they serve as life-preservers—as if I am alone, floating in a stormy ocean and there—there might be land. I open them cautiously, letting them sit for a day or two at first to make sure they are not contaminated, they are something to look forward to, a reason to go on a little longer. Find out what's in the box.

Fabric masks from friends.
Masks from former dress designers.
Snacks, dried fruit and nuts and granola.
A care package from my Husband.
My favorite coffee from my mother-in-law.

Each is a reminder of a time before. I bring the cookies my cousin ships me to work to share with the staff—she has packaged them individually in plastic bags so they are easy to hand out. I still eat more of the cookies myself than I care to admit.

23.

I t is remiss of me to talk about my time there without mentioning the exceptional staff who worked at the hospital—I have made wonderful friends. We have cried together, held hands, and held vigils for patients taking their last breaths. I have met nurses of the highest caliber in this situation and I could not have survived without them. I have also met some spectacular physicians and residents, some wonderful therapists for the patients—but I could not have survived without the nurses. We are holding the line.

Many of our patients will go on with us for months, some hospitalized 30, 60, 80, 90 days. They become our families, more so than our own. Collectively, we love them, care for them, soothe their families, hold their hands. There is no cure. We wait in hope that their medically induced comas will help, that they will survive long enough for us to find anything that works. Our hope, like a candle, is dampened, gradually, while we watch them all go through the same setbacks. Respiratory failure, kidney failure, sepsis, heart failure, clots, infections, we call this multi-system organ failure. We are somber in our expectations —but there is still hope for us, yet.

There is a patient named Fred who has been with us since the beginning. He is relatively young, only 50, with no pre-existing conditions. His nurses and physicians are hopeful; we tell each other Fred will be our miracle. We get him enrolled in the plasma trial, in drug trials. Cutting edge treatments, we will try anything to get him through this. By rights, if anyone should survive, it should be Fred.

His adult daughter calls every day.

We prone him, a team of 6 people gently supporting him, rolling him inch by inch onto his belly so his lungs might oxygenate better, a respiratory therapist at his head controlling his neck and ventilator.

He stays on his belly for 18 hours, his oxygenation is better, we un-prone. His face is swollen but he is stable.

His oxygenation levels drop.

We re-prone him urgently and joke maybe he is a belly sleeper. The subtext, we are afraid.

His clock ticks on, Fred will live another day.

24.

I care for one patient for weeks, John, every day pending extubation, every day the answer is one more day, from the physicians.

Today, I beg them.

I know they don't want him to fail extubation and set him back but we need this and so does he. We have two Recreational Therapists on our unit, holdovers from the old psychiatric unit. They have spent the last two months in every capacity except the one they signed up for, most recently they gown up and schedule Facetime calls with families since we still do not allow visitors. They will do calls with John and his wife every day, bent over the bed, holding the tablet close so families can see the faces of their loved ones, stroking their hair. John's wife is very religious and will assure him she reads Psalms every day for him, she has been using the "healing oil" every day, in the hopes he will come home.

I wonder what healing oil is and how you use it kind of idly, but not enough to ask. I think at this point, I'll take all the help I can get.

We extubate him and he is placed on oxygen support—but he is not re-intubated for now. It is a success. He is still confused, lethargic, but he seems to be holding on and is more alert every day. I see our recreational therapist there with him, holding the tablet up and I realize he will talk to his wife for the first time since he has been intubated.

I hear days later John will be downgraded to a regular floor—he is a success!

I have to say goodbye, to see him before he goes, and I stop by his room when I have a moment to spare. I am excitedly telling him what a miracle he is when I realize he is looking at me, bemused, as if trying to place me. He seems confused by my enthusiasm for his miraculous improvement.

I apologize. *I'm sorry, you probably don't remember me. I was your nurse while you were intubated for weeks.*

John smiles. *No...I remember your voice,* he tells me. His hair is gray and white, wild, his beard is scraggly and his voice hoarse. In this instant he is angelic. I let the relief wash over me. Just for this moment, through all of the misery and struggle to keep them alive, this moment I have helped.

Someone made it. I assemble the few staff members I can round up to be his honor guard and we clap and cheer for him as he is wheeled out of the ICU. He is one of the few we are able to extubate that does not require reintubation.

25.

I go home, shower, and then sleep soundly. The subway vibration feels like a lullaby in my floorboards, and suddenly it is morning again. I am awake in the early morning sunshine and I go to the park to spend a few hours walking. With the sun on my face and the slight breeze, I am grateful to be alive.

I go home, shower off my sunscreen, climb into bed. The afternoon sunlight pools on the white sheets, soft and clean, I am bathed in sunshine. It feels luxurious, the light filtered through the shades on my face, my hands; I feel cat-like in this moment, warm and safe, I stretch. I see the shelves on the wall to my left, they have four glass bells on them, blue. The light catches the blue glass and I think to myself that I understand why it feels like home.

26.

My favorite patient is Henry. I have only ever known him while he is awake, he has COVID-19 and has been intubated and successfully extubated. He is mentally handicapped, childlike, with Downs' Syndrome and—to be honest, a light for us in the darkness. He lives in a group home, he has for years, but he wants to go back there, so it seems like they must be good to him. Henry is short, frog-legged, he is strong. His skin is marred by a handful of scars, sutured, he has had surgery before. He is brown-eyed, joyous. He dances with us. He colors with us. He laughs and makes his needs known and has a return to baseline functioning (minus his lung status, which we were sure would improve)—as soon as we could get his lungs well enough not to need oxygen, he could go back home. Although he is mostly non-verbal, limited to only a few words, it is easy to understand what he wants. I estimate his mentality to be in grade school, perhaps between

6 and 8 years cognitively, although it is not my specialty—maybe I do not give him the credit he is due. He gestures for things, points, and it feels like we play a days-long game of charades in which we both win. He understands much more than most people expect.

While he might be initially resistant to something if it was not what he wanted or was not comfortable, if I explain to him why we need to do it, he will cooperate. He struggles with the fine motor coordination to feed himself, but would dab his lips with a napkin to make sure there was nothing on his face. I care for him for weeks, too, and he is another symbol—Henry is *success*. Although physically, he is older than me, due to his cognitive abilities and our interactions he feels like the son I have not yet borne. I could have a son that age.

The physicians "downgraded" him to a lower level of care, a medical-surgical floor. I beg to keep him in the ICU even though I know it is selfish. We need him—we all did.

I packed his things and explained to him that he is being transferred and he says, *No*.

I apologize, *I'm sorry Henry*, and continue to remove his cardiac monitoring equipment.

Henry begins to cry and strike out at me, but when he sees he cannot stop me, he relaxes. I am holding back tears and when I am finished, he says, *sorry*, and reaches his arms out to me for a hug.

I hold him for a moment, say goodbye, and let the transporters wheel him away. I am worried that the nurses who take care of him on other floors won't know him as I do, won't have the time to understand him as I can. I stop myself. I have to trust in the inherent goodness of other nurses. They will. Everyone who has met him loves him.

It is a good thing, the resident reminds me. *He is well enough that he doesn't need to be here.*

I know. God, does my head hurt.

Fred is still with us, our miracle-to-be, like a cat with 9 lives, we are uncertain the plasma has had an effect of any kind. He is still enrolled in the drug trial, anything cutting edge we can get our hands on. We are watching the monitor when his blood pressure spikes and then drops. We check his pupils. One dilated, one pinpoint. Fred has had a stroke. We cannot confirm it with a CT scan because our portable CT scanner does not fit in these rooms, and he is not stable enough to move.

He lives another day and all of our hearts break for him.

27.

My husband sends me a Mother's Day package, which I find on my doorstep one day after work. There is a card, a love letter inside. He always tells me that he is not a writer, he chafes at the idea of written affection —but I wish I could tell him that to me, he is a poet. I trace the words with my fingers, re-reading them, I feel closer to him seeing his handwriting on the page.

In the box, there is a picture frame. There is no photo, just a white piece of paper. He has traced their paw prints, perfect, in different colored markers, and I wonder how he made them so even. Green for one dog, purple for the other, he has written their names underneath. I run my fingers over the glass, I think of our dogs, of home, and I sit on the floor in my kitchen.

I think of our adopted family, the college team we used to coach, and the young adults that still call me *mom*. Softly, I think of pastel blankets and of cribs. Longing isn't the right word, but it's the closest one I have.

The box has a candle, hand-painted, it is beautiful. I open it—it stinks like cheap pine air fresheners. I laugh out loud. He picked it out himself.

28.

Today I am taking care of a patient named Harriet. Harriet is intubated but we are waking her up, and she may be extubated today. She is 70, but a good 70, she looks like she could be 20 years younger. Dark-skinned, her kinky-curly hair is tied back in a pony-tail, shot through with gray but not yet having lost the darkness from her youth.

She has been in a coma for a month, probably. She is still not awake, although her sedation has been off for over a day, which worries me. I ask her to squeeze my fingers, my hand in hers, I am hesitant. There is a pause. I ask her again, louder, hopeful.

Harriet, Squeeze my hand. Squeeze for me.

Her fingers twitch—is it a curl? I ask her to wiggle her toes, to be sure.

A twitch—one foot.

Again, Harriet, Wiggle your toes for me.

She does. I am elated.

The attending physician wants her to be more alert. We will wait another day. Another day. Another day. A week passes.

29.

I receive a few messages from a work acquaintance who owns her own ballroom studio
on the other side of the country—she wants
to hire a teacher through our company, this is
strictly business.

We connect originally over work, but over emails
and texts we become fast friends. She reminds me
of the older sister I never had, she is so generous
with her time and energy. She asks for my address;
she ships me a box of skincare products with instructions, so thoughtful, comments like *Good for
PPE face* and *To look like you're well-rested. HAH!*

My heart feels raw at the thought she put into this,
printed instructions with flowers, there are comments on every item (2-3 uses. Once a week).

I am touched, genuinely. We have planned on having lunch at every national competition for the
last six months—all canceled. We have never met.

Exfoliating? Serum? Ideas so foreign at this point, self-care sounds like a foreign language.

I realize how long it has been since I tried to take care of myself, how bizarre this ritual feels. I think of leaving sacrifices, gifts, to statues for good harvests. As if we could appease the universe in some way, us humans, tiny in the scheme of the galaxy, we think ourselves so complex. I think if I could leave an orange to a clay religious statue and the next day the pandemic would be lifted, we would have a cure, I would do it.

I feel more human. I follow her instructions, I exfoliate, I tone, I moisturize.

The whole city is closed. It's something to do.

30.

I am working two days later when we get an admission that sounds familiar—it's Henry, the patient I just downgraded, and my heart drops so low it might have shattered on the ground, if that kind of thing was possible; I am on a roller coaster and the bottom has dropped out, I feel fragile, I do not know if there is a safety net. I feel sick. I am due for the admission, as if fate has conspired against me. I know I do not want it, but I also know that I do not want him to be without me, so deeply protective of him do I feel.

I prepare his room. IV pumps ready, plugged in, extra tubing for the pumps and labels. A blood pressure cuff, disposable, for the monitor, a pulse oxygen sensor, electrodes for the ECG monitor. Socks.

He is brought up to the unit still awake—although I know from the report he will likely need to be intubated again as his respiratory status is compromised. He sees me in the hallway from the gurney and visibly sighs relief, face relaxing, he tries to smile. He waves at me, still struggling to breathe, but happy in this moment that I am here, and I am fighting back the tears as if he is my son. In this instant, I know I am unworthy of the trust he has placed in me, the way he relaxes when he sees it is me, but I am desperate to deserve it. I know how this will go from looking at the pallor cast on his skin, the way his shoulders retract while he tries to breathe. I know how this goes.

His only IV that he comes up with from the medical floor doesn't work and my hands are shaking while I place a single IV and get it—on the first try —although his veins are incredibly difficult due to his anatomy. My hands are shaking harder the second time and although I try, I can't get the second line I know I will need. Henry is crying and begging me to stop, the needles, they hurt.

I talk with his resident physician this time, a reasonable, brilliant woman who shares my first name, and she loves him as I do. She tells me she knows he will need a bedside procedure of central lines including an arterial line to monitor his blood pressure closely and a central line for IV medication and blood draws; the peripheral IV I inserted will not be enough access for all of the medication and monitoring we will need. But, she tells me, she also knows he will probably be sedated for his intubation and she doesn't want it to hurt—better, she thinks, to wait until he is sedated so he won't feel any discomfort.

I am at his bedside for hours holding his hands. I am singing. I am talking. I am rubbing lotion on his dry hands and feet. I am doing anything I can to prolong this moment but he cannot hold on to his tenuous breathing and he must be intubated to save his life.

He is afraid, crying through his BiPAP mask sitting up in bed, he has been through this before. He leans into me, hugs me and I hold him while he cries. I realize my mask is wet because I am crying too, ugly crying, and I can't stop. I promise him he will be safe, I will keep him safe, it's not going to hurt.

I know I need to be strong in this moment, for both of us. He does not have the reserves, he is not strong enough to struggle anymore for air, he has none left he can draw on, his lungs are heavy with fluid. I can feel his sobs against my body, feel his lungs vibrating against his back. The anesthesiologist arrives to intubate him and is in position at the head of the bed, headboard removed, the physicians look to me and nod. I lay him down into the bed, still clinging to my arms, and they hand me medications to push into his single good IV to sedate and paralyze him so we can intubate him—standard procedure. The doctors take the sheet and slide him up in the bed towards the anesthesiologist, waiting, with his tools, with an endotracheal tube that will pass into Henry's throat and down, deep, past his voice box where it can push air into his lungs.

This is all standard but I can't shake the feeling of *away*; as if, somehow by virtue of shifting him closer to the anesthesiologist they are in some ways taking him from me. I am crying so hard my goggles have fogged up and I remove them so I can see what I'm doing.

The residents ask me if they should go get someone else but I shake my head and try to stop the tears streaming down my face. My hands are shaking while I inject the medication he needs. I give him the gift of sleep.

I love him in the only way that I can. I label his IV lines. I wash his face. I prepare the drugs and label and sign and date and time and initial them all in a row—I bridge the compatible ones while I wait for the physicians to place a central line. I fold the sheet at the bottom of his bed and position pillows under him.

The attending physician is older, she has done this for so many years she has a daughter by the same name that is also a physician at our hospital. She says to herself, as if she is alone, that he will not survive. Softly, she regrets this, but her experience is guiding her judgment. I must have made a noise, although I do not remember speaking, because she turns and sees my face.

She says she is sorry. She wishes all her patients could have a nurse like me.

I feel woefully inadequate. Shame. I understand that there is nothing I could have done, that it was out of my hands, that this was the right decision for him at this time to prolong his life. I feel guilt. I nod dumbly because I don't know what else to say and I don't trust my voice. When I walk out into the hallway, several of my coworkers, now friends, see me and stop their charting. They put their arms around me and I shake. My eyes are red and my mask is wet. There are maybe two or three of them surrounding me and there are arms around me on all sides. They know how I feel and I try to focus, to somehow channel the pressure of their arms on my skin into strength, as if I could recharge myself like an old battery. It's too much for any one person to bear.

I see the doctor that was with me in Henry's room, in the hallway outside. I apologize for crying. I know it's unprofessional.

She swats me gruffly with her hand and tells me not to apologize. She hugs me. I have never seen her affectionate, not even with her daughter—maybe in her mind, it is a sign of weakness.

She looks in my eyes.

It was the right decision. She tells me. *He needed this.*

The way she says it, it sounds like she is asking my forgiveness.

I know, I tell her.

I go home and take my shoes off in the anteroom. In front of my door, there is a plant—lilies, Easter lilies? They are yellow like sunshine, in full bloom, potted so they will last as long as I can keep them alive. There is an orange thank you card tucked into them from my landlord.

I feel the tears well up and I wonder what the odds are that today is the day he would leave them for me.

I shower, scalding hot, trying to scrub the day from me as if I can wash it away. I feel the cotton sheets on my skin, close my eyes, and I sleep. The train probably still passes by underneath me, but I don't notice.

31.

I take care of Henry several days after this with the same unwavering meticulous attention. He loves music, so I play music in his room and sing to him. I sit with him for hours when I am not busy with other patients. There is one day that we have the staffing to make him a 1:1 due to the acuity and I spend 12 hours in his room. I learn that he oxygenates better if he is positioned with his left lung down, lying on his side. Sometimes, his blood pressure will drop and I will talk to him again and it will rebound. He doesn't want to be alone, I think. He is critically ill but I think he might be getting a little better. There is a respiratory therapist who I have worked with before a few times. He is a little older, a father, with a shaved head and sleeve tattoos I sometimes see when it is too warm outside for an under-shirt. He is an excellent therapist and he is most often the one I call on for help in an emergency, even if it is not his patient or his problem, and he will always come. His name is John. He often will tell me, Look! Little man's blood gases are better today! He will get Henry a pediatric mask from another part of the hospital because it fits better, John will go above and beyond and I think he loves Henry as we all do. John provides the same unwavering support for all of his patients and I felt safer knowing he is involved in Henry's care.

My friend Yana is working today, and she comes to the room to ask me a question. She sees Henry, takes my hand and his, her question momentarily forgotten.

Dear universe, Yana starts. *There has been so much death and we will bend to your will but please, do not take this one. Please let him live. We need him. If you have to take him, please help us understand. Amen.*

I am not a religious person by nature, and under normal circumstances I might feel silly. Yana's words, like a prayer she is offering from within to whoever is listening. Yana is normally well-spoken, but here she struggles to find the words. I wonder if Yana's religious leanings are fumbling, new to her. I decide I don't care, I am grateful for this kindness. In this moment, I think I'll take all the help I can get.

I go to work. I come home. I smell the coffee. I think it smells right. I realize the lilies will die, here in the darkened apartment all day, so I drag a stool out over to the windows on the right side of my living room that face the street.

I open the window shutters so they can get the sunshine. I am not good at keeping plants alive but this is the only other living thing in my apartment and I am determined I will. I go back to work.

32.

Due to staffing, I am shifted around the unit to other patients for a week or two. I know this is probably for the best. I am too close, I care too much about the outcome of this case and it will consume me, it will eat me alive. I see John but he does not mention Henry.

One of my patients today is Derrick. Derrick is a huge person, football player huge, 6 and a half feet tall, easy. Young, as far as hospital patients normally go, he is probably 50. He is 400 lbs of muscle, strong and dense, and it takes a team of 3 or 4 people to move him so we can clean him and turn and position him. Derrick has been here maybe a month, he is intubated and sedated like the rest of them into a medically induced coma. His wife is a police officer, I think. She is incredibly kind and grateful.

Derrick has so many IV pumps running medications that I have to keep at least 9 or 10 spare bags of medications ready. Insulin. Versed. Fentanyl. Precedex. Calcium Gluconate. Heparin. IV antibiotics. Sodium Bicarbonate. Levophed. Electrolytes, Magnesium, Potassium, there are so many, on, off, on, off.

His kidneys are failing so we dialyze him and the resident, Ben, is very involved. Ben loves Derrick like I love Henry, and I respect him for it. I think, in retrospect, all of us had one like Henry.

I flush his dialysis lines, they are in his neck, so-called temporary, acute lines, we hope his kidneys will recover. I get a dialysis machine from a unit downstairs, I drag the dialysis fluid from the supply room—40 liters, it is heavy, I bring 10 liters at a time. I run tubing, the waste line, under his bed, to the bathroom, I tape it to the sink. I set the machine to prime, I prepare the dialysis bags on the machine, I prime the dialysis fluid line—there can be no air in the lines or it will be forced into his arteries—he could die.

I connect the lines, the tubing, to him, One line to draw blood and one line to return it, I unclamp everything and cross my fingers and watch, nervous, as the machine draws, the cloud of red filling the lines.

The pressures look good, everything is working, and I monitor his blood pressure closely while I adjust the amount of waste fluid the machine will discard according to the nephrologist's orders. I adjust his Levophed for blood pressure and I wait, his guardian at the ready to stop things, to titrate his medications, to rinse his blood back if he cannot tolerate it.

Everything is fine.

I care for Derrick for days and by the end of it, we are hoping to extubate him tomorrow—but I am off, and I will not be here to celebrate our victory. His kidneys are improving, I have been able to wean him down off several medications he needed the first day.

Ben looks forward to telling Derrick's wife the good news and he sits down outside the room, where it is quiet, to call her. He is focused, quiet, he gives her his undivided attention. His voice is kind, soft, he is cautionary, he is hopeful but tempers her expectations. He does not want to let her down.

Ben looks up at me, after. *She is the only person I say, 'call me any time.' I mean it. 2 am, she could call me, I wouldn't be mad.*

Ben stands up. He is taller than my husband, with good posture, dark-haired, and brown-eyed. He is an ER-resident and I feel confident that he knows what he is doing. I like working with him because he listens to me and I think he genuinely cares about his patients.

We want to get a CT of Derrick but we cannot fit

the portable CT scanner in the room. He is stable enough, we think, so he is transported downstairs with a nurse, respiratory therapist, physician.

He cannot fit in the scanner.

I am so frustrated that we cannot get a CT scan of him. *What would we do normally?* I ask. There's got to be a way. *Don't we have a bigger scanner?*

One of the residents says that sometimes we take patients to the zoo.

You have got to be kidding. It strikes me as funny, somehow, that this giant hospital system does not have a bariatric scanner, that the only way to get this scan is to transport the patient to the zoo, how ridiculous is this situation, we would have to mercy flight him across the city for a *zoo*?

I laugh, out of control, but it is the tired, bizarre laughter you might hear from a psychiatric ward in a movie: a brain misfiring, mirthless. I am not laughing at Derrick, I am laughing at how ridiculous this situation is because if I do not laugh I might cry.

She's not kidding. But they won't take him because of the ventilator: He's not stable enough to transport across the city.

33.

I have worked with Dan, one of the former psychiatric nurses, a couple of times.

He tells me that all the former psychiatric nurses are frustrated about the loss of their psych unit (understandably) and are being redeployed as medical-surgical nurses indefinitely. They did not sign up for this, but some take to the new responsibilities a little better than others. He is working across the hall in the next unit. He asks me to come supervise him with an IV—he can do it, but he hasn't done it in years. He doesn't feel confident.

Of course, I say.

He probably would be fine if he had to figure it out by himself, but I like Dan. He has been a nurse for decades, only most recently doing psychiatric care. While he does not necessarily remember exactly what he has learned about medical nursing years ago, he has the right instincts, and I trust him. I make sure I tell his patient what a great nurse he is, how lucky they are to have him. He smiles at me under his mask, embarrassed, but pleased.

I go home. My landlord has left me a bottle of hand sanitizer, lavender-scented, on the shelf.

My head is killing me.

I see Harriet again, assigned to her for the first time in weeks. Like many of our patients, she has struggled to wake from her medically induced coma. We don't know why we can't wake them up. I suspect, out loud, to a group of residents, that perhaps they are having micro-strokes. We know there are micro-clots. Is there brain damage?

One shrugs. *Even if they were, we can't CT scan them*; we can't transport them and the scanners don't fit in our rooms. It would not change our course of treatment in most cases. What could we do?

Another looks more curious. *Maybe they are*, she says.

The attending physician at the time, the same long, lanky woman with wild curls, tells me she doesn't think so. I trust her implicitly.

Due to the fear they would need to be re-intubated, the fact that we cannot leave them intubated this long, Harriet has a tracheostomy. We tried, for a long time, to avoid tracheostomies in these patients. They walked into the hospital with a cough. It seems so permanent, this scar. They could recover, be extubated, any day. The problem is that people are not meant to be intubated for long periods of time; due to the pressure of the endotracheal tube and the balloon to keep it in place, patients begin to develop tears, holes, in their tracheas. Stretching. Fistula. Endotracheal tubes we use to intubate begin to leak air and need to be replaced. The physicians start performing tracheostomies. It seems to be our best bet to keep them alive.

Harriet opens her eyes when she hears the door close in the room. I ask her questions, she answers with a nod or a shake of her head. She still cannot talk due to the ventilator attached to her tracheostomy. I ask physical therapy to see her and, with their help, she sits on the edge of the bed. I am managing her ventilator, one physical therapist is in front of her, and one physical therapist is behind her, supporting her.

We ask her how she feels and I can read her lips when she tries to say, *It's been a while.*

We laugh, together, this tiny victory is ours to hold onto; I kiss her hands through my mask and she smiles at me. She is backlit by the window behind her, sunlight streaks the silver in her hair. In this moment, she is angelic, eternal. Harriet becomes synonymous with hope. She begins the process of the extensive physical therapy she will need to go back to her life. Lift your leg for me. Higher. Flex your toes forward. Now towards you. Pick up your other leg. Harriet will make it. She is 70 years old, but she will make it.

I go home. I can still smell the coffee. Relief isn't exactly the right word, but it's close.

34.

I am walking into the residents' room to ask a physician for an order one night when one of them says he thinks three patients will die tonight. I ask who—one of them is Henry.

No! I say. *I saw him yesterday, he was fine!*

He shrugs. *Go look at him.*

I have to.

I sit on Henry's bed and reach for his hand in the darkened room and I know they are right. I don't know how to explain a nurse's intuition about death. I feel, again, like we are the gatekeepers —as if we can look at them and know an invisible clock has almost struck midnight. We have an agreement—we will never hasten that time—but we will stand on the edge of the abyss with them and hold their hands while they pass through. A squeeze, a release, a brush of fingers slipping away. They are gone.

I look at his face, eyes open but unseeing. Tongue protruding. He looks so much like a macabre caricature and unlike himself that I focus down on his hands, instead.

I hold his hand, crying again. I tell him how grateful I am for the joy that he brought us and how sorry I am. I tell him we know it is time and we know he is tired. I am sorry I broke my promise. I weep over his hands while I tell him I understand, and it is okay to go. I understand that there is nothing we can do for him at this moment and all I want is to know he will not suffer. I leave the room sobbing—I can hear his clock. I know he is a full code and we will have to perform chest compressions even though I do not think he will survive. He is only 35 years old.

People seem to think that CPR is a magic bullet—that somehow someone who is so near to death that you can hear the clock ticking—will magically be saved. In many cases, we cannot convince a stopped heart to beat. It is an old law. An object in motion will stay in motion; an object at rest will stay at rest, especially if that patient is critically ill. Everything that is left is trauma for the patient and the provider.

I see one of the night nurses on the way out who knows how much I care about his case and will try to assign me to him if she can. She is witty, sharp, quick to laugh and remarkably kind. She has been the monitor nurse for the last several weeks at night because she injured her hand, and she's not supposed to have direct patient contact until it heals. I am always pleased to see her, glasses and ECG patterned scrub cap, and she greets me with the same enthusiasm.

Sarah, I say, thickly. *Please don't let him suffer.*

I don't know what else to say but she feels the sorrow in my skin. I know this is an unfair request—of course she cannot change the code status, she cannot stop it. It is unjust to put this responsibility on her. She hugs me, and there is sympathy in her eyes. She doesn't have to say anything. She will do her best.

I wake up in the dead of night—I dream of wings, of *nothing hurts*, of peace, and I know Henry is gone. When I get to work they only confirm what I already know and I numbly think about going home sick before I start my shift. Sarah says she is sorry and I shake my head. I know it is not her fault.

My back hurts. Everything is sore. I'm so tired.

35.

Fred, our cat-with-nine-lives, our miracle in waiting, is imminently dying. We are all dying, in a way, I guess, but his clock has begun to tick louder and we know it is almost time. He has had at least 2 strokes, we think, it might be 3. He is still in a coma. The physicians call his adult daughter to come say goodbye. She comes in, we fit her with a precious N-95 mask, a gown, gloves. I apologize to her. We are sorry we couldn't do more for him. We have tried everything we have. She is gracious, although I am sure she does not hear me.

We are allowing visitors now, 15 minutes, only if the patient is actively dying. A resident I have never liked very much has been taking care of Fred and he waits for Fred's daughter in the hall. He is probably a good doctor, but I tend to avoid him because I usually find him condescending—but I have never seen him like this when he stops her outside her father's room.

He will not look like you remember him. Your father is very sick. He is swollen from fluid, he is in a coma, he has been through a lot.

The tears start in tracks down her cheeks, she is softly weeping but does not lose her composure. I am impressed by her strength, sincerely remorseful for her loss. We have all cared for her father over the course of his hospital stay, all of our hands have carried him this far. We think of him as our own.

The resident takes her hands. *He is still your father. This is only the shell that is holding him. Say goodbye, but remember him the way he was.*

I decide in this moment I like the resident more.

At the monitor, I watch her in her father's room. We have given her a chair, but it is not close enough for her. She stands at her father's bedside, stroking the hair back from his face. She holds his hands, she leans down to his face so he can hear her better. She presses her forehead to his and clutches his hand to her, and I know in this moment that Fred was a good father.

Ellie, can you come help us with this blood work? She's a hard stick.

Sure, Dan. I don't mind—in fact, I am grateful to be useful to him. I prefer the distraction of helping out with another patient, the work, even if it does not belong to me. It feels good to have a reason to walk away from the scene playing out in front of my eyes and not have Fred's final moments with his daughter imprinted on my memory.

It is the beginning of a day in which 9 patients will die on my unit, including Fred. Can you hear the bells?

I see Ben, the tall resident, walking out of our unit tonight after he has signed over his patients to the night team. Ben looks heavy today, unusual for him, he hangs his head and his shoulders are slumped. It is almost our shift change, but I am caught up on my work for the moment.

Ben.

Ben, what's wrong?

He looks up at me from the floor, pauses in the doorway.

I think Derrick's going to die tonight.

His voice cracks and I can see the tears in his eyes. You can smell the guilt on him, the stink of misplaced failure, of shame. We are standing in the hallway, him half out the door.

I know it is not his fault but he feels it in his bones, he cannot shake it, the idea that he might have missed something, there is something he could have done differently, that he made the wrong decision.

Ben, I'm sorry.

I am helpless to provide comfort.

He nods, he has no more words that are safe, he cannot meet my eyes, he slips out the door and is gone.

36.

People are saying on the news that the numbers in New York are looking better—our hospitalizations are dropping! Fewer new cases! Look at the promising metrics!

I want to scream at them that it is only because most of our ICU patients are dying and the city is closed so there are no new infections. I wish they could hear the death clock almost audible to us, to bear the sadness that we do knowing we are powerless to stop it in this case.

I wonder if they would still think the numbers looked better, if they would still brag about metrics. I am afraid, and it is not the first time.

People say we are heroes now.

Healthcare Heroes! Heroes work here! Signs proclaim all over New York City with a single exclamation point, they shout about their heroes. They are talking about us. The first time I heard the roar outside, I thought something must be wrong. A nurse directs me to the window, indulgently, and I look outside to see the chaos.

People everywhere, standing in doorways, leaning out of apartment windows, on balconies, they cheer for us at 7 PM every night. Shouting, clapping, they bang on pots and pans like so many children in the kitchen with wooden spoons. Every night, it goes on for months. 7 PM, like clockwork, and all at once they begin anew.

They only make me feel guilty, these faceless, nameless cheers. If truly, we were heroes, we would be able to take care of them better. We would have answers. We wouldn't be missing... something. What are we missing? Why can't we stop this? They wouldn't keep dying.

People wouldn't accuse us of leaving patients to die, of faking the pandemic, of lying about the numbers for money. *Heroes.* Do heroes fail you so catastrophically? When I see them, instead of feeling supported, feeling appreciated, I feel ironic. I feel shame. I feel guilt.

I walk past them, head down.

I hold onto our successes, our patients, in my mind as the lighthouse in the distance, in the dark. They remind me how close we are, we must be to land, to safety, if only we can stay afloat.

Harriet has made it out and gone to a rehab.

143

John left and went to a medical-surgical floor.

Madelyn went home.

Laura went to a rehab.

I say their names on bad days like a prayer. We tell their stories amongst ourselves when the burden feels too great. They are our heroes, our miracles, our reasons to continue when we feel as though we cannot go on doing this. For this one person, we made a difference.

I wake up, I fill the French press. I can still smell the coffee.

37.

I go back to work. Laura has had a stroke at her rehab facility and she is back. It feels like a sucker punch to the gut, the idea that somehow out of our hands we have still failed her.

It feels like a light that was burning has begun to sputter out. When I arrived, I told my patients, *Not today!* As in *You won't die on me, today!* and I meant it. And for the most part, while I feel that some may have sustained on my sheer force of will and determination, they lived another day. There is a study I remember, from back when I worked on a cardiac floor years ago; researchers have found that even when you control for all variables, patients who report believing that their nurses and doctors cared about them, believe in them, will have better outcomes. I wonder idly if that applies here, to medically induced comas and a disease for which we have no cure.

I begin to feel listless. I see them for what feels

like the first time. I see their suffering—that many of them have no hope of a meaningful recovery, that many of them are trapped in their own bodies and there is only the suffering of the ICU. A nurse I work with says to me,

The only difference between what we do to people in the ICU, and torture, is intent. If we are causing suffering in order to save their lives, it is medicine. If we are causing suffering because the family wants to prolong their life—even though there is no hope of a meaningful recovery—it is torture.

I am more measured now, and it feels in some ways more compassionate. I know that for some of these patients who will never see the light of day again that the best thing that could happen to them would be a good death. I advocate more strongly to physicians and residents to discuss palliative care for patients that will never return to their lives, brain-damaged and ventilator dependent; I wonder what kind of life this is for anyone.

I hold their hands and I tell them it is ok if they are ready. We know they are tired. We know their families love them. No one wants them to suffer.

I hear the clock tick, softly, and instead of feeling anxious I am peaceful, resigned.

Most of them die very shortly after that conversation, making me believe even more strongly that they can hear us, even in that state.

A family we have advocated strongly with makes the decision to terminally extubate their father, Hank, who will never recover. We will "pull the plug," so to speak. I ask them when they will arrive, assuming they will want to spend his last moments with him, but they tell me over the phone that they have said their goodbyes over Facetime and they don't want to be here for this.

I can't help but think of people who have the veterinarian euthanize their animals but won't stay with them, and there is a lump in my throat. I do not blame them for not wanting to remember their father this way, I only regret the situation we are in and I think of Hank. I assemble the respiratory therapist, resident physician, and I prepare an IV drip of morphine so that he will not feel any pain. I find a playlist of music from the '50s and '60s, when he would have been in his 20s and 30s, and I play it on my phone in his room. Our protocol is to disconnect the ventilator but not remove the breathing tube due to the risk of aerosolizing virus particles. The respiratory therapist disconnects the ventilator and the resident pauses, surprised.

What if he doesn't go right away? He asks. *Can we just remove the tube? I don't want him to be uncomfortable.*

We understand this is not the protocol, it puts us

all at higher risk for exposure to the virus, but I hear the genuine concern in his voice and we agree, it is unanimous. The respiratory therapist pulls the breathing tube out smoothly, wraps it in a towel to be disposed of in a biohazard bin.

Hank breathes on his own, heavily, labored, but he draws his own breaths. I adjust his pain medication until he looks comfortable and he does not visibly struggle for air.

I sit down and hold his hand. I imagine he and his wife dancing to the music of the times that I hear in the room—I wonder if they danced at malt shops and held hands and shared milkshakes before they married. I wonder if that is a stereotype, but I decide I don't care. I imagine her with a poodle skirt and a ponytail, manicured nails drumming along on the table while she waited for him to ask her to dance. I think of Christmases with their children, toddlers with bright wrapping paper and indulgent smiles over their heads, of Easter egg hunts and birthdays and family dinners. I imagine him younger and vibrant and full of life.

I wonder if your life flashes before your eyes at the end, your eyes only, or if it plays like a movie reel and if only someone cared enough to watch, they could. I stroke the top of his hand and wonder how close I am to the truth, about the kind of life he lived. It doesn't matter.

Hank holds on for nearly two hours. The resident stands vigil at his bedside with me—at 7 PM it is time for him to give signout to the next shift and leave, and he tells me he will. My respect for him deepens when he comes back after his shift and waits with me. Standing there in the silence between us, he says his father was terminally ill in medical school and he had to make this decision. He is calm, there are no cracks in his voice or face but I can see clearly how this has tempered him like scorched steel in water. I begin to understand his quiet concern about removing the breathing tube so that the patient would be completely at ease. I know when he finishes his residency he will be an incredible attending physician someday. For the first time—instead of his first name, another resident, in my mind I see the doctor he has already become.

I imagine this same vigil for his father, but I know he was there.

I watch Hank's heart rate begin to drop with his blood pressure and I know it's time. I think that the last thing I want is for him to die on a commercial break or to *Rockin' Robin*.

I play *Hallelujah*, acapella, and by the first chorus he sighs and does not draw another breath.

Time of Death, 7:08.

Our resident thanks me, and he leaves. I do not

know how deeply he felt this, but he is stoic. I have wept.

I am walking out of the room when I see the resident from the night Henry died. Clearly looking for me, he hangs his head and he tells me he is sorry. I cannot process, I think he must know that Hank has just died, and I blindly thank him.

He ran the code, he did the best job he knew how to do, but we couldn't get him back. He confides in me that he doesn't feel good about it, but he does his job. He goes back to the residents' room, afterward, and throws things; he wants to break things, overwhelmed, there is no other way for him to express how he feels about what has happened.

It occurs to me he is telling me about Henry's death, he doesn't know about Hank, and I try to jerk myself back to the present moment. *Thank you*, I say, *I know*. He shakes his head and wanders off to see another patient, but I can tell he is sincere in the way he carries himself, slumped and repentant. He feels like he let us down. I wonder how much invisible weight he carries, like all of us, on his shoulders.

My head hurts for days.

38.

Gradually our staff travelers on shorter contracts begin to leave. I am stunned by the resilience of the human spirit—not only in our patients that have survived this long in spite of many setbacks, some of whom having been hospitalized for as many as 60 or 80 days —but also of the staff who have survived this so long. Hank's doctor told me he saw 300 people die with his own eyes in March, at the height of the pandemic, ER packed full of people, codes run constantly, beds in the hallway because there was nowhere to put people—I wonder how much suffering, how much guilt, any one person can bear.

I see the resident from my first day in the hallway. She smiles when she sees me and asks how I am. We briefly chat and she asks if I heard the news.

What news?

Nevermind, she says. Her face falls.

No, tell me.

Madelyn was discharged. Then she died. We thought she would make it.

George calls me after work one day, he wants to talk about anything, God is he lonely. He has been quarantined at home for months. I am having a bad day, and I mention it, briefly.

It feels like I worked so hard, before, so many hours. Now that I am here, it just seems like it was all for nothing.

There is a pause.

Someday, George tells me, *all the stories of your life and everything that you have been through will come together, tied up in a bow, and you will understand why they happened to you. My mentor told me that.*

39.

W hat started as peaceful protests over the murder of an unarmed black man by police officers have turned into full-scale riots at times and in some places due to police brutality at the protests; as well as other instigators starting looting and fights to discredit the whole movement. The original protestors, I think, were shoved to the side by those who were looking for a fight. The riots begin in some parts of the country. New York is one of those places.

There is a curfew enacted after 8 PM and I hurry home every day after my shift, not wanting to get caught in the crossfires. One day I am walking back from an ACLS certification class, a requirement for me to keep up as an ICU nurse, when I see a school of police cars. I think to myself, with the lights flashing, a school, I imagine fish—I don't think anything of it. *A school, that can't be right*, I am amused at the bizarre tricks your brain will play when you are overtired—I can't come up with the right words, but I don't care, and when I turn the corner I am absorbed into a wall of thousands of people.

How do you spell Racist, They chant. *NYPD!*

I can't breathe! I can't breathe!

Hands up, Don't shoot! Hands up, Don't shoot!

I am near tears. I am afraid, overwhelmed, guilt-ridden; it is loud. I am claustrophobic at this moment and I can't get out. They are peaceful, they are chanting, but there is a deadly respiratory virus that is spreading and the last thing I want is to be surrounded by shoulder-to-shoulder people. They are everywhere—in front of me, behind me, packing the sidewalk and covering the street, they move as one unit—I am panicking internally but I cannot push past them, there are too many and they are packed too tightly and there is a wall to my left side and after a block or so I am able to get out to the street, which is full of stopped traffic—but at least I can get away from all of the people. I feel almost like a traitor, but how different is shouting, chanting, from coughing? I support their message and what they are trying to do —reform systemic racism and brutality that has gone on for years—but I am too afraid to be caught up in it if it turns violent.

At night, although I live in a so-called nice neighborhood, I can hear helicopters, the launching of tear gas canisters, and gunshots. I feel guilt that perhaps I am not doing enough by working in the ICU, that maybe I should help the protestors, could I offer them a safe place to hide until the curfew is over in the morning?

I am a woman living alone in New York City, every fiber of my being is remembering the questions I do not want to answer should something happen to me—*So, you let them in your home, knowingly?*

I think of every criminal justice show I have ever watched, of assault, it doesn't matter who they are, I do not open the door to strangers. This goes on every night for 10 days in my neighborhood. *Survivor's guilt* isn't the right idea, but it comes close.

In some ways, while I watch the news and see the current events unfolding, I am taken aback. There are so many things happening—the protests, the police brutality, a particular kind of insect they have dubbed 'murder hornets', science-denying, spikes in pandemic cases.

It feels like the only thing happening is COVID-19. Everything else happens in the background of this huge, overarching theme. I don't know how to cope so I stop watching the news regularly.

I am bitter.

I can still smell the coffee.

40.

A nurse I work with, Yana, has befriended me throughout the long days here in New York. She is away from her boyfriend back in Texas, and while she loves Houston she is a lovely ex-pat that immigrated here many years ago. Her accent never quite adopted the southern twang you'd expect for a woman who says she is from Texas, but her enthusiasm and energy were infectious and part of her charm. I have worked with her in several situations and I know she is the kind of nurse I want to be—she is the nurse that said a prayer with me for Henry. She knows what she is talking about, her patients are always pristine, clean, and tucked in and safe. She is always kind to me; funny and brilliant are defining characteristics of hers.

Yana is the kind of person that would accompany me to the bedside of a patient near death and hold a vigil and say a prayer—even if it wasn't her patient or mine.

She is charming when she asks me to cut and dye her hair, which is how I ended up in her apartment, only a few blocks from my own, mixing hair dye and attempting a haircut with layers I have only watched tutorials of on YouTube. I want to go to a beauty supply store and get toner, so her hair is blonder. It feels very important to do a good job, for some reason, although we wear scrub caps over our hair every day at work. She doesn't want to put any more chemicals on her hair.

No one is going to see it, anyway, She reminds me. She dries it, curls her hair, and I am struck by how beautiful she is. I have worked with her for months and I have never seen her hair or, it seems like, the bottom half of her face. Logically, I must have seen it, but I see her so much more often fully masked and gowned up that I have not associated the face with her.

We laugh and eat sushi at her kitchen table, light streaming through the windows, and it feels momentarily like a reprieve from the situation, from our lives. I watch her particular way of lifting the fish off the top of her sushi roll, spreading wasabi on the rice, and putting the fish back before eating it. I have never seen anyone do it that way; I remember my husband smoothing wasabi over the top with his chopsticks, and it doesn't matter because I don't even eat wasabi.

We paint our nails at the kitchen table, file them, and I am struck by how normal this feels, considering we work in a post-apocalyptic war-zone some days.

Yana is not a difficult person to be around, she is constantly engaging and a witty conversationalist.

I allow myself to think of how nervous I was about spending time with anyone outside of work—that there will be nothing left of me to give, socializing will be too hard. Relief isn't the right word, but it comes close.

She is thrilled with the haircut—*Remember, the bar is low!* She tells me, and later, *Don't worry, I won't let my hairdresser talk shit about you.*

She asks me to come to the park with her because a resident, Vlad, a first-year, has asked her to come spend time with him. She wants to make friends but she doesn't want him to get the wrong idea— she has a boyfriend, and she doesn't want Vlad to misunderstand her intentions.

He seems slightly put out that she has brought me but I know him and we have worked together, we are amicable. They want a drink so we stop off at a store and they each buy some booze—I buy some Chex mix and dried pineapple. Under normal circumstances, I might have felt silly, but I still don't drink and for some reason, it doesn't feel like now is the time.

We sit on a bench in the park and Yana and Vlad talk about their families, about what they think the meaning of life is, about patients, and what we could do better. I chime in occasionally and share my Chex mix, but mostly I listen.

I am watching the fading light catch the ripples over the lake, the slight breeze whispering through the long grass.

I realize it is getting dark.

We have to go, guys.

I see people walking by with signs for the protests, I know it is getting dark and there will be curfew soon—is there still curfew? I do not remember, but it seems very important that we are not out after dark, and I do not want to be arrested.

It sounds like an adventure, Yana says.

Then you can stay, I tell her. *I am leaving.*

Yana and Vlad walk with me. It seems like darkness is falling much faster than I thought. The trees loom ahead, normally I enjoy the shade but now it feels foreboding and claustrophobic, a canopy that might close in. Yana is a little tipsy and she complains about how fast I walk.

I tell her, *It's because you have to project your body*

forward. Push forward with your steps, not up. She links arms with me.

Ah! She says. We power-walk together, Yana giggling softly, with Vlad trailing behind on his cell phone.

We pass my apartment and I open the gate.

Come with us! Yana says. *We will get Thai food and sit on the steps outside.*

I can't imagine being out with the threat of the protests looming. Also, I don't even know if I like Thai food.

I am exhausted from all of the socialization. I thank her but go home.

41.

I miss my husband as if I am missing my own shadow. There is a space beside me that feels empty. I reach for a hand that is not there. Sometimes, it seems like he exists on the periphery of my mind, if I only do not look for him, he might be sitting on the couch, watching the news —but every time I see something out of the corner of my eyes I turn to look, and there is no one in the apartment but me.

We plan a flight—I have three days off in two weeks, he can come to visit on my days off, and I am giddy with excitement. I have not seen him in two months. I thought for some reason I would be able to go home and visit when I came here, but there is a quarantine in place. If I come back from out of state travel, I am supposed to quarantine for two weeks, right? He would have to quarantine, but since he is furloughed and cannot work it doesn't make much difference for him. There seems to be no timeline on when the economy will re-open and he can go back to work.

I did not anticipate a situation in which I would not see him for months when I took this contract. In some ways, I am glad, because every week I do not see him is another week I do not have to be afraid I will give him this virus that has taken over my life.

The date is fast approaching and I am nervous. *You have to wear a mask,* I tell him. *I will wear one too. The whole time.*

He does not want to, he is bold, unafraid. He tries to poke a hole in my logic, in my plan to protect him from me, in case I am an asymptomatic carrier.

Will you wear one when you sleep? He is asking me, amused, with disbelief.

Yes, I say.

He says stubbornly, *I'm not going to fly 1300 miles and not kiss my wife.*

I say, *Then don't come.* Resolute.

He hears the fear in my voice. He acquiesces. He is not afraid, but then again, he has not seen what I have seen.

The weekend before his trip our bosses tell us that they think the studio will be able to reopen next week.

My husband is afraid, for the first time. *What if I get sick?* He whispers into the phone.
I tell him to cancel his trip. I feel hollow saying it but I know it is for the best.

The studio is not allowed to open, and we find out the day after his original flight was scheduled to arrive at the JFK airport.

We book another one.

My skin aches for touch. It has been months since anyone touched me or I have touched anyone else without a gloved hand. I am hungry for skin like I might be hungry for a meal in a way I cannot explain. I want nothing more than to sit in front of my husband and feel the contours of his face with my fingers, as if I am blind and this is the only way I can see him. I feel some days like a shell—devoid of a human inside, I wish for touch.

42.

I go back to work. The days blend together until they tell me I can't work any more overtime and I am relegated to my four shifts a week. I spend some days being the meticulous nurse I want to be. Some days, I begin to understand, the best I can do is keep them alive. I am at peace with that as long as I know I did the best I could.

It is 7 PM, nearly the end of our shift and I am walking out of a room, when Max, another nurse, comes down the hall looking for me. *Ellie? Yana needs you. Now.*

I hear the urgency in his voice and I run.

A patient Yana is very attached to emotionally, one she has taken care of for weeks, is on the edge of a cardiac arrest and there will be no intervention fast enough to save her. We assemble the critical care team and the crash cart and within minutes we begin chest compressions.

The patient has been hospitalized for at least a month, ventilated and sedated, she is elderly, and her chances are not good after her most recent deterioration. After about 10 minutes, there is a pause in the attending physician's speech. He is thinking about the patient's chances. About her odds of brain damage. About conserving resources. He hesitates for seconds when someone asks him a question and Yana and I can feel that he is about to suggest we end the code. Yana looks up at him, her voice high and tight, and says, *Just don't give up on her.*

The decision is made for him in her statement, as close as Yana would come to begging in that moment and we code her for another 40 minutes. We get a pulse back momentarily, but have to code her again and after over an hour and a half she is stabilized, her heart on borrowed beats that we have given to her, for now. Our shift has long been over, and I place my hand on Yana's shoulder. *I think we should leave*, I tell her. I know how this goes and I can feel the quiet desperation under her skin.

I'm okay, really, she says, fiercely, as if she is brushing my concern off like dust from her scrubs, and we both know she is lying but we finish our documentation and leave.

Yana is flying home this weekend to visit her boyfriend in Texas. She breaks down crying at the airport but she comes back better, closer to the Yana I know.

I begin to walk in the park on my days off—I set my goal at 30,000 steps. It takes me hours, and I while them away, listening to late show after late show. Colbert. Noah. Oliver. It's the only way I can stand to hear the news, lately.

By the time I get home I'm too tired to feel very much. It seems like an improvement.

43.

One quiet, pleasant day on the unit my patient has been seen by the wound nurses and they have recommended for her a specialty hospital bed that will decrease the pressure on her skin.

I say quiet now, in hindsight, because no nurse will ever use the phrase "Quiet," to describe a shift that has not yet ended. It is a surefire way to tempt all hell to break loose.

The bed arrives the same afternoon and I enlist the respiratory therapist and my helper, Maggie, who is a brilliant nurse, funny, kind, and patient. Maggie is a little older than me, not by much, and came here with her husband, who is a PA. They have an infant daughter. She is the hardest working person I know and will often be found cleaning and organizing supplies in my patients' rooms. When we work together, which is rare, it feels like I have become an octopus—I will be saying something and she is already doing it before I get the words out, as if she can read my mind, we are an extension of each other. We often will leave music channels on the television in the patients' rooms working together—we know they can hear, we assume it must pass the time for them, too, and it distracts from the sometimes inhumane job we must do.

We move the bed as far over into the tiny room as we can and bring the second bed alongside it so we can slide her over. She is a tiny woman, and the respiratory therapist is managing her ventilator while my helper and I will slide her over into the new bed and we can reposition it to take the old bed out. The furniture is stacked and while we seize fistfuls of the sheet to shift her into the new bed gently, the song that comes on is *Toosie Slide*.

We are laughing, the three of us, together in this too small, too hot, too busy room, at the coincidence. I am climbing into her bed, ducking under her ventilator tubes and out of the space the headboard is missing from, to unplug the old bed so we can move it out of the room. There is a weightlessness for the moment, a frivolity, that I cannot explain.

44.

It seems like a joke when the next day a new bed comes for Derrick, our football player sized-patient who did not die the night Ben thought he might. His clock has not yet run down.

I am hopeful that Derrick will actually make it. Ben was wrong about that night, and Derrick seems to be improving. He is young, yet.

I assemble a team of 8 people to move him onto the new bed. It is a disaster, the bed so big and so many people in the room, but Yana comes to help and she is somehow able to direct the traffic effectively in such a way that this 400 lb man ends up safely in his new bed and we get the old bed out. I go to ask Ben for an order in the residents' room, it is late in our shift. I am wearing clean isolation gear, ridiculous, but it's the style these days—I was gowned up to go into the room and remembered I needed something from the doctors.

The residents introduce me to another doctor I do not know, he is filling in today. They tell me he is a former professional salsa dancer from Puerto Rico, he came here for his residency, and they look back to me, expectantly, almost hopeful. Some-one changes the television to a music channel—it is social Latin dance music, I am still here and he offers me his hand almost hesitantly. He is unsure if I will take it, but I do.

We are dancing, strangers, but in this moment we are one. Sneakers on carpeted floor, I remember what joy is—I don't even like the style of dance the music calls for, but in this moment I do not care.

It has been months since I got to dance with any-one, my isolation gown is like crepe paper it is so light, it is tangled around me and I am laugh-ing, joyous. There is music, there is rhythm, and in these precious seconds, there is nothing else.

Jake opens the door to the residents' room. *Ellie, we need you.*

We got thirty seconds, maybe a minute, of this dance, but I am still flushed, embarrassed that Jake has walked in on this. Jake is indulgent, he pre-tends not to have noticed, the resident I danced with squeezes my hand and lets me go.

45.

It is almost June. Other states are beginning to reopen, which I warn everyone I can talk to will go terribly in a few weeks.

Please, stay home if you can. Stay safe.

I feel like I am standing on the beach watching the tsunami coming towards me—knowing it will wash over me but also knowing that I am powerless to stop it, like the tide.

At first, I am concerned. I think about the loss of human life. The unnecessary exposure of hospital staff to more patients than we can handle, the illness and death of hospital staff that will surely follow. The death toll of civilians. I am heavy and sad with the grief for what is to come.

My head hurts again.

I walk to the dry cleaners on my day off to discover the one I have been going to, half a mile away, is shuttered. There are no signs, but it is empty. I carry the twenty pounds of laundry back. On my way home, I notice the dry cleaner closest to my apartment is open for the first time since I have lived here.

I am getting ready to cross the street on my way into work in the morning when I am joined by another nurse in scrubs headed to the hospital. We start to cross, the light changes and someone honks at us—we are closer to one side, so we step back out of the street.

Remember when we were heroes? I ask her. *They would have stopped traffic for us.*

We laugh together, strangers, but in this moment, sisters.

46.

They reopen in phases.

My husband flies in and calls me when he arrives at my apartment. I have worked all day and it is late but I am waiting, showered and dressed in pajamas, hair washed, there is no part of me that has not been washed from the hospital so there is nothing I am bringing to him on my clothes.

I see him standing outside my gate, under the street lights, and he looks like a stranger. The moon is full—he might have asked me, in the time before, if I thought it was waxing or waning, but I can never keep them straight no matter how many times he explains.

It feels strange to let him in, as if in some way I am cheating on him—him, my husband, whom I am letting inside. I can't quite explain how foreign it feels to let another human, a man, into my apartment.

I have picked up sushi ahead of time and we eat on the couch, not at the table. We are relaxed and I watch him, his mannerisms, the way he moves his fingers, the way his face looks when he laughs.

I can't put my finger on it but something about his face, his body, his hands, something feels off. I want to trace his face with my fingertips and mold my body to his so I can memorize the way he feels again. It seems almost as if I have betrayed him, as if my memory is only a terrible, quick charcoal sketch I did of a masterpiece in a museum and how little justice I could do to the lines of his body compared to the original. I think, briefly, of art classes in the time before. Figure drawing classes composed of dozens of people in a room, easels close together. How strange it seems, the idea that we could all be together in an enclosed space, so near to each other, and not be afraid.

Our first day I wake up early, we are walking to the crepe store around the corner that is now open for takeout. I take him to the park and we sit in the grass in the warm sun and eat our crepes. I want him to see everything I have done in Brooklyn so far, to share with him.

He doesn't want to carry his coffee, but I don't want to sit anymore, so he drains it in one long swig and I laugh. Problem solved.

We hold hands and walk in the park. This is my tenth week. I get a call from a place I applied back at home—they want to interview me, can I come this week?

I schedule the interview for Thursday, my last day off, the day my husband is supposed to go home. I am so relieved at the idea that I might get to come home and stay home.

I take him to the hospital and we walk around the outside. To the dry cleaner. To the grocery store. Any place we have talked about, I am desperate to share this life with him and still feel like we are in sync, like this is our life, instead of just my life, alone. We get pizza and go home. I fall asleep in his arms and all is quiet.

The next day I have planned to take him to Roosevelt Island, an islet in New York City with an abandoned smallpox hospital and an air tram, my friend Amy has told me. I have never been.

We take the subway, I lend him my Metropass to get through the gate—I am a real New Yorker now, he doesn't need to buy a one-time card—and nearly 40 minutes later we are on Roosevelt Island. We walk out of the subway station and see the river in front of us. There is a path with a rail —the water is fast-moving, but it is beautiful and the sun is shining. We walk to the tip of the island —there is a lighthouse, hand in hand. I am nervous about my interview tomorrow but he reminds me that even if I don't get it, we have lost nothing. Fingers interlaced, it is easy. I am so glad I married him.

Our afternoon is cut short when we realize due to the lockdown there are no public bathrooms.
We wandered the shore for a couple hours but never did make it to the air tram or the hospital.

Thursday morning we are up early, flying into Miami together. My husband has downloaded a show on Netflix and we spend a few hours together, quiet. It reminds me of all of the traveling we used to do for work prior to this—of the time before. I remember business trips, blazers, red lipstick, mobile hotspots, and business cards. I hardly notice my mask anymore.

At the airport, there are National Guardsmen handing out contact tracing surveys about quarantines. They politely enforce the line and do not allow travelers to pass unless they have turned one in. I am shaken to see the army fatigues at the airport—it seems so post-apocalyptic—but at least they are trying.

After the interview, I come home and my dogs are in a frenzy. My husband jokes about how he is the one that fed them for two months and you'd think he wasn't here.

I laugh and spend a few blissful hours at home

—my husband orders takeout from one of my favorite restaurants and we eat on our own couch, home together at last, if only momentarily. We take a nap in bed, the four of us, my husband, the dogs and I, and it is the best sleep of my life. Peace is almost the right word. I feel rested for the first time in months and I do not dream.

I work the next day in New York, so I fly back to JFK the same night. I am tempted to stay home, to quit my job, to stay with my family. I get back on the plane even though every fiber of my being tells me to stay—every fiber of the universe, it seems. My Uber gets in a minor car accident, my plane is nearly grounded. I make it back to my apartment, somehow unscathed.

I go to work. I can still smell the coffee.

48.

I meet Josephine. Josephine is a sweet, shriveled raisin of a person, absolutely beautiful in the way that a grandmother might be. Her family calls often and they leave me with no doubt she was a lovely wife and mother—they are as loving and sweet as I imagine she must have been. Josephine's death is imminent, and at this point we are still allowing visitors to come in for 15 minutes at a time, to sit by her bedside, and to say their goodbyes. Her daughter is a nurse practitioner and tells me they want her to go to hospice. Her husband accompanies their daughter, his cane and unsteady gait betraying just how difficult this must be.

He presses his forehead against hers and whispers to her. It feels too personal, a lifetime of memories, and I slip out the door.

When their time is up, I gently come in to escort them away. Josephine's husband, Alex, stands tall and takes my hands in his own.

I have been with Josephine for 57 years, he tells me. I want to take her home. Please. Let me take my wife home. I just want her to be with her family. There are tears in his eyes and soon they are standing in mine. I will try, I promise him.

I walk them to the elevators, a woman on a mission. I call around to find a social worker or discharge planner who can help us. She has a hospital bed at home, they told me. We just need oxygen.

The social worker is on board to help but feels handicapped because Josephine needs oxygen and does not have oxygen at home. It is 5 PM on a Sunday. She will not be able to get a vendor open to bring oxygen to them on a Sunday night.

I know Jo's time is almost up. I can feel it. I call her daughter and ask her if she can get oxygen tanks from work. She will try, she says, desperately.

I am afraid that Josephine will not make it through the night. Tomorrow is Monday. We could make all this happen on Monday.

Jo quickly deteriorates and I call the nursing supervisor and ask permission to let the family come back and stay with her. I feel her death is imminent and she will not make it home. The nursing supervisor says he will look the other way and I leave a nurse at Josephine's bedside while I am getting ready to go get the family from the hospital lobby. Jo's blood pressure begins to drop, scary low, I know she cannot sustain life like this much longer.

I look at the nurse I have left at Jo's bedside.

If she dies before they make it back here, you turn that monitor off.

It must have just happened, I tell her. *When they got here.* The nurse looks at me, first in disbelief, and then in sorrow, but she nods.

It is a lie, but a kind lie, and I have an accomplice. I will tell her daughter the truth and let her decide if she wants to tell her father or not.

I feel like I am racing the clock as I run down the stairs to the lobby. I gently take Alex's hand and he walks with me while his family trails, daughter, son, grandson. They are crying. Her daughter has prepared them. Her husband does not cry.

I open the door—Josephine's monitor is still on. I breathe a silent prayer of forgiveness to whoever might be listening for the lie I didn't have to tell.

They will stay with her through the night and Alex will go home to get his morning medication, as he has been here for more than 10 hours.

The next morning, I come in—Josephine has hung on. She waits until her husband comes back. He is holding her hand, forehead to hers, talking to her gently in the way you'd talk to a loved one in bed. The bell tolls—chimes, for her, I imagine—and she slips away.

I give him a few minutes before I help him up. His tears have run tracks down his cheeks and now seeing this stoic old man cry, I am crying too.

He hugs me and tells me, *God Bless you. She was lucky to have you. You are our angel.*

My chest feels a crushing pressure, a weight, as if it is being sucked down to my feet. *I'm sorry I couldn't get her home,* I tell him. The guilt pours off me like cheap perfume.

He pats my hand. *You're a good girl. You did the best you could.*

I tell him, *I hope my husband loves me someday the way you loved Jo.*

Alex smiles. *Why wouldn't he? You're a good girl.*

After I talk with Jo's husband I think about my husband. We have only been together a handful of years but when I remember him now all I can remember is the way he makes me feel. I don't even remember what we used to fight about.

I have always resented it when people memorialize those that have died, romanticize them and forget all their flaws. It makes them less human, I think. Makes it seem like they weren't good enough the way they were. You miss someone they are not.

I tell myself that maybe we aren't intentionally de-humanizing our loved ones, but the way they make us feel colors our perception of them. He loved Jo and that love so far outweighed anything else they may have been through in 50 years that all he had left was their love story, their family, the happy memories she had given him. I decide that it's beautiful for the first time in my life.

49.

I am back at work, assigned Derrick's room, I assume we will need to do dialysis today. I go in to do my morning assessment and see another patient. I am glad she is asleep so she cannot see the look on my face.

I find the charge nurse.

What happened to Derrick? I am frantic with a mixture of hope and fear.

Derrick died overnight two days ago. Grains of sand, slipping through the hourglass, silently, quietly, there is no clock, there is only the softness of sand rushing through and then...nothing.

I see Ben, the resident, later but never again on my unit. I won't tell him about Derrick. I know how it feels.

I am exhausted, as though my light has finally flickered out. I watch the cases of Coronavirus in other states climb—it's all there is on the news. I expected I could go home at the end of my contract and back to my life, but it is readily apparent to me that I will be flying out of one pandemic and into another. I tell my husband, grimly, to stock up on non-perishables. I am furious. They don't believe us. They don't believe it is that bad. They don't take it seriously. They think New York has overreacted.

The unnamed *They* has taken the place of all of the faceless, nameless people driving up the cases in other states with risky behavior, going to parties, and refusing to wear masks. I settle into seething that the general public would do this to us, again—the reopening of states, too fast, the huge spikes in cases. People protest mask-wearing and mandatory closures. Signs at a protest read ridiculous, *I need a haircut!*, as if that is at all relevant if thousands of people will die because salons and non-essential businesses are opened before we can contain the virus. Hospitals are quickly becoming overwhelmed. *Healthcare Heroes*, indeed. I feel betrayed.

I mentally prepare myself for the onslaught of those first weeks. I cannot stop it from happening again, and I am furious. Let them come.

50.

I have taken care of Peter on and off again for the last two months. He is ventilator dependent, and in our estimation, all but brain dead, in multi-system organ failure. We have tried to talk to Peter's son about his prognosis, but Peter's wife has died of multi-system organ failure in the last year. He is unable, like many, to reconcile the idea of the man that is left with us, to the man that raised him his entire life. Peter's son wants us to "do everything," although Peter is in his 90's with advanced dementia. We are saddened by it and many physicians and nurses have tried to gently educate him on the fact that Peter would probably not survive such a situation—Peter's son cannot fathom.

So Peter has a tracheostomy placed.

Peter's kidneys fail, so we have to place dialysis lines in him and begin dialysis, some weeks nearly every day. He appears to be essentially hanging in limbo.

He has been with us 60 days, at least. His eyes move around the room, but he does not track people in the room or turn his head to us when we speak to him. He does not follow commands in any way, but he blinks and coughs.

I try to gently talk to Peter's son, again, about his father. Peter's son becomes angry when I ask him what his goals of care are.

It's just because you don't speak to him in Russian! he insists. *If you'd only speak to him in Russian. He has dementia, sure, but he understands.*

I apologize and end the call as quickly as I can. It is apparent to me that he is not ready—but ok, I'll bite, I think. What can it hurt? I go to Peter's room, take his hand, and speak the few Russian phrases I know.

There is a pause. He stares, unblinking, into the distance.

He makes a honking sound at me, and I wonder, sadly, if this is what Peter's son meant.

I don't know what I was expecting.

51.

Amy has also been a good friend of mine throughout my time in New York—she is a long-distance runner, beansprout small and wiry in the way of a person that can eat an entire pizza and still have chiseled abs. I mean, probably—I never saw them. She is a capable, intelligent nurse, often echoing my anxieties and fears out loud. I soothe us both by reminding her of the reasons our anxieties are not real or reasonable. She is a staple of my time in the city, a traveler, like me, she has left her husband behind at home and she is from Kansas City. She is sweet and often bubbly, if she was a drink she would be champagne —often a shoulder to lean on or extra hands to lighten the load.

There is a day my patients are relatively stabilized and she seems frazzled, hurrying by me on our regular unit. *Amy*, I say, *Let me know if you need anything.* I am catching up on charting in the hallway, and she doesn't even slow down.

Thanks, She says, gowning up to go into a room that contains a COVID-19 positive patient. The door hasn't hit the frame yet when my walkie crackles.

Ellie, I need you.

I hear the urgency and the hair on the back of my neck stands up. I am still pulling my gloves on while I get into the room. *Amy, what do you need?*

I see her patient—intubated, paralyzed, sedated, oxygenating poorly, and with a steadily plummeting blood pressure and heart rate. I grab the crash cart outside the room and, at a heart rate of 30, Amy slams an amp of epinephrine into the patient's IV.

I know this patient is dangerously ill, her advanced directives are full code, and her daughter works here. She is in multi-system organ failure and is almost certainly close to brain-death due to our struggles to oxygenate her no matter what we tried during the course of her illness. I personally have begged her daughter to think about changing her advanced directives one day I cared for this patient—she will not survive a code, there is nothing we could do to pull her back, so close to the edge of the abyss. Her daughter cries in my arms that day, and I cry with her, distance be damned. I am hopeful she will change her mind, that I have gotten through to her, but she cannot. *I don't want to be the one that kills Mom,* she says.

We try to educate her, gently, that we will not kill her mother if she is a DNR—we will treat her up to the moment her heart stops. Do Not Resuscitate does not mean, *Do Not Treat*, it means no heroic measures that surely will not save her mother. We cannot save her mother from this.

She is resolute, though, *Do everything*—and we must, knowing as we do that it is futile, inhumane; we will do our jobs even as it breaks our hearts.

Her heart rate climbs again as the physicians begin to arrive and we roll her to place a backboard so that we can do chest compressions if she drops again. We whisper silent thank yous to whoever might be listening, we tell ourselves, *Not today.* The resident and Amy wait by her bedside for hours, standing silent guard, as if by virtue of their bedside vigil they could will her to live a little longer. Her clock has not yet run down, incredibly, and Amy finally leaves the room for the first time in hours.

I am sitting at the monitor when I watch Amy walk into her other patient's room, another intubated, sedated man on a ventilator.

She is still there when his heart stops and he begins to alarm "asystole"—a flat line.

The seconds last for an eternity, my hand on the

code alarm, I am watching her on the monitor. Amy sees him, shakes him, she hopes it is not real.

James. JAMES. JAMES, WHAT THE FUCK! She shouts, a normally good-natured person she is stretched to the breaking point and the strands have begun to snap.

She seizes another vial of a rescue medication, she will not lose this one, and as she turns back to him, his heart begins to beat again. His heart paused, it lasted for seconds, but today was not the day for his clock to run down—he is not yet out of time. We laugh about it later, a little darkly but mostly relieved we did not lose another one.

Well, hell, if all else fails, try yelling at them. It hadn't occurred to us to try that, but nothing else works.

52.

L ater an acquaintance says, It's such a shame about the looting.

One of my close, dear friends that I have known for nearly 5 years and has been like a son to me is Jamaican—I coached a college team years ago with my husband, and he is one of the team members that has since gone on to graduate. He and his fiancée send me Mother's Day cards every year to this day.

I think of hosting the team at our house for dinner, pounds and pounds of spaghetti and fifteen or twenty college kids gathered around my dining room table, my couch, they spill over onto the floor; of traveling with them out of state to competitions, getting up at 3 AM to do hair for the girls dancing at 8 AM. Although they are not so much younger than me, I am a mentor, their away-at-college mom, and they are in some ways the children I have always wanted but not yet had.

When they called me, *Mom*, the first time, we were in a store and they were calling my name across a crowded aisle, but I did not hear them.

One of them called out, *Mom!* She was joking.

Inexplicably, I heard it and I turned around. It stuck for years.

My Jamaican student, his skin is so dark and I realize for the first time in my entire, selfish life that any of these situations with unarmed black men dying at the hands of police officers could have been about him.

It's such a shame about the looting, my acquaintance says again as if I did not hear her.

It dawns on me that I would burn the entire city to the ground if it meant that I could protect him from this and I say,

Don't you mean it's such a shame that people have to destroy property to be heard about the deaths of innocent people at the hands of police?

I won't even begin to address the fact that in some places it is suspect that other groups that were not a part of the movement have come in to stir up violence and discontent, to discredit the protesters.

I can hear my heartbeat in my ears and I realize I am angry, so angry my hands are shaking. It could have been my son, the one I have not yet borne, or the one I have adopted from our college team so many years ago.

I think of the man most recently killed by the police, one of his last words, *Mama,* and I think all mothers are summoned when he cried out for his.

53.

I am taking care of Peter today, again, my Russian patient, and he has taken a turn for the worst. Peter's blood pressure is dropping, his oxygenation is dropping, and in spite of my best efforts to reverse him, stabilizing him seems like a joke because it appears that this death is inevitable.

I know he is tired. I know I am tired. I know what we have done to him in the name of keeping him alive is unfair. But I won't give up on him today. Today is not the day.

I spend hours at his bedside adjusting medications, calling physicians, repositioning him, calling respiratory therapy, trying anything we can to improve his vital signs. He looks gray.

It's only 5 PM, there are nearly three hours left in my shift. I cannot explain my desperation in this moment to keep him going just a little longer; I am frantic not to lose another patient I have worked so hard to keep alive—for months! I will not lose another one.

I get into his field of view, where I can see his eyes, although I am uncertain they can see me.

YOU LISTEN HERE, I tell him. I have SLAVED over your body for MONTHS and I am NOT going to let you die on me today. I KNOW you're tired. I KNOW you're ready. I am off tomorrow and if you want to go tomorrow I will understand. But NOT TODAY. Do you hear me? NOT TODAY.

The clock continues to tick, momentarily, minutes from midnight, my reprieve has been granted, he lives on borrowed time. Peter will go on to live through the rest of my shift, the evening shift, and die the next day.

Maybe in that moment, he could feel my desperation not to lose another one—but he held on for me.

54.

I begin to have patients that are COVID-19 negative and awake in some cases. It is June. I feel like I have to recalibrate when my patients are awake and want to talk to me—I haven't had patients that wanted to talk to me in years, it seems like.

My unit is almost devoid of all of our original COVID-19 patients. Almost all of the ones I knew died, or the two or three of our original 30 that have lived this long have begun to test negative—although they may have "recovered" from coronavirus they are profoundly disabled—brain dead, or very near to it, in some cases, dependent on ventilators and feeding tubes. This is what recovery looks like.

Our studio owners email my husband and tell him our furlough is indefinite. It has become much more important that I find another job. He does not have health insurance and very soon, neither will I. I cry because although this was not unexpected it feels like a loss. I could not envision a future after the pandemic in New York that I did not get to go back to my life at home.

I imagine going into practice with George at the studio at 10 AM even though we don't teach until 12. I imagine the light streaming through the windows, the pristine sun-kissed floor, the crystal chandeliers.

I can hear the music. I stand in front of George, and as one, I move towards him, compressed, he catches my hips and suddenly I am above him, hands on his shoulders I am 10 feet in the air, we are balanced. I twist, I roll my left hip into his palm, begin to stack my body over this one arm, in his hand, this lift is called the star. In this moment, aloft, I am flying. There is a momentary wobble, we overbalance, I fall, George catches me and I laugh. George has never dropped me.

I imagine dancing with my husband, one of the days we feel really connected, we are able to execute beautifully in-sync and the music seems to be controlled by us, instead of the other way around. We waltz, we are light on our feet, there is a growth of our movement, we harmonize. We are one. George is watching us together, this section of our routine is new, we ask what he thinks. He is crying. He remembers where we started and how far we have come.

I imagine our coaches, working through a particular movement or expression, getting it right.

I remember the look on the audience member's face—he was my student—when we danced into the corner at a performance, a competition. I am close enough to touch, my line extending only inches from him, I see his face. Awe. Admiration. It is seconds, but we have locked eyes and it feels eternal.

I cannot imagine that we won't go back.

We begin to look at the process of opening our own studio when this is over. Rise up.

It seems to be a futile idea. *When this is over*. It feels like this is how it has been for years, that my romanticized memories of dancing before work with the sunlight streaming through the windows —of the audience applause—of things less than life and death—were a dream, a temporary reprieve from the inevitable.

55.

I begin to have nightmares about patients in impossible situations. Patients I cannot save, patients that attack me somehow although they are intubated and sedated they are somehow awake and I wake screaming still feeling hands around my throat while I am trying to save their lives. Some days I see my coworkers or friends in the dark, their faces melting from their bones in some macabre skit I struggle to put from my mind.

The days blurred together when I arrived, moments into hours into days.

It is my last week of this contract and all of the moments that seemed on fast forward when I got here have been added to my last few shifts, as if sand has been added to the hourglass in the final seconds.

The days are eternal. I am watching the cases tick

up at home in Florida, and I know I am flying home to another pandemic. I hope I will get a week at home before I have to walk into another hospital just like I did in April—it feels like a hellish version of Groundhog Day.

My lilies have stopped blooming but they are green, shoots healthy, there are leaves reaching to the sun. I leave them on the stool by the window for the next occupant of my Brooklyn apartment.

Tomorrow is July. The new residents begin, hospitals at home are quickly reaching ICU capacity and they have just canceled elective surgeries; 5,000, 9,000, 10,000 new cases a day.

Where was I...?

For Karen, Kendra, Mallory, Enrique, Michael, Maria, Josephine, Sparky, Paulette, Julie & Senta

For Jessi, Jeremy, and Justin, who listened to me.

For Dr Sury, and baby Sury, Nibs, Elizabeth, Sarah, Ilya, Eric, Dr. Minkin, Kika.

For Ben, who taught me about Vents.

For Kaitlyn, who says I am *her* nurse.

For Dima, who taught me to dance.

For Paris, Andrea, and Carly who made me laugh and shared the dance floor.

For Iris, who taught me about blood gases and A lines.

For Keisha, who can find *anything.*

For Laura, who taught me about a Fluff and Puff.

For Kayla, who I trusted implicitly.

For Carrie, who kept track of all of us.

For Yara and Anthony, who taught me about everything else.

For Jason, who taught me to fly.

For Akeem and Victoria, whom I couldn't be more proud of.

For my husband, Vincent, who told me, *You have a book here, you need to tell this story.*

Made in the USA
Columbia, SC
19 July 2020